Isaac Backus
and the
American Pietistic Tradition

William G. McLoughlin

Isaac Backus
and the
American Pietistic Tradition

Edited by Oscar Handlin

Little, Brown and Company • *Boston*

LIBRARY OF CONGRESS CATALOG CARD NO. 67-19143

B

*This book is affectionately
dedicated to
Louise Day Duffy,
an indomitable exponent of
the free human spirit*

*Published simultaneously in Canada
by Little, Brown & Company (Canada) Limited*

PRINTED IN THE UNITED STATES OF AMERICA

Editor's Preface

THE AMERICAN REVOLUTION was far more complex than most historians have supposed. It not only dissolved the ties of empire and touched off a reordering of all social relationships within the new nation; it was, in addition, a revolution in the hearts and minds of the people who participated in it. The last-named aspect has only slowly begun to become apparent.

That the Revolution was related to intellectual developments in the eighteenth century was long since clear. The Declaration of Independence itself spoke of laws of nature and its rhetoric corresponds to the theories of the Enlightenment. But the emotional and religious strand in the rebellion has not been so clear, either to participants or to the scholars who later examined its course.

William McLoughlin's vivid biography of Isaac Backus throws light on the developments which imparted a religious dimension to the struggle for American nationality. Already in the seventeenth century, the colonists had worried about the obligations imposed by conscience and the relationship of the individual to society. That anxiety grew deeper in the eighteenth century.

Isaac Backus grew up in an environment which repeatedly thrust those problems upon men's attention. He lived at a time when religious issues raised the question of where the true source of spiritual authority lay, whether in the church or in the individual conscience. Significantly, just then also, social and economic changes raised parallel questions about the nature of secular authority. Backus and his Baptist following wrestled with both sets of issues; and the course they took as the Revolution unfolded would have a permanent effect upon American character and institutions.

OSCAR HANDLIN

Contents

Acknowledgments

First I wish to acknowledge my debt to the staffs of the John Carter Brown Library under Thomas R. Adams, and of the Brown University Library under David A. Jonah, for their unfailing and unstinted cooperation in providing me with books, manuscripts, ideal working conditions and expert bibliographic advice. In addition, the staffs and resources of the following libraries deserve special thanks: the Massachusetts Historical Society, the American Antiquarian Society, the American Baptist Historical Society, the Connecticut Historical Society, the Connecticut State Library, the Rhode Island Historical Society, the New Hampshire Historical Society, the New York Public Library, and the Harvard University Library. The friendly cooperation of Ellis E. O'Neal, Jr. and the Andover Newton Theological School and the generous gift of Backus papers by Miss Florence Backus of Riverside, California, were absolutely essential.

At the risk of unfair and unintentional omissions, I wish also to thank the following individuals who, at one stage or another, have assisted my research on Isaac Backus: Lyman H. Butterfield, Malcolm Freiberg, Stephen T. Riley, John D. Cushing, Clifford K. Shipton, L. Kinvin Wroth, Mrs. Elliot Perkins, the Rev. G. Oliver Donner, the Rev. Nelson R. Elliott, the Rev. Homer C. Bryant, Edward C. Starr, Thompson G. Harlow, Wesley G. Dennen, John Lundvall, John M. Bumsted, and especially John Walsh of Jesus College, Oxford, who read and commented on the entire manuscript.

And last, but not least, special personal thanks are due to Oscar Handlin for his wise counsel and expert editing and to my wife, Virginia Ward McLoughlin, for sharing the general burdens of a scholar's life.

Grants from the following sources aided me greatly in various aspects of this study: John Simon Guggenheim Memorial Foundation, the Harvard University Center for the Study of the History of Liberty, and Brown University.

WILLIAM G. McLOUGHLIN

PROLOGUE
The Pietistic
and the
Secular Traditions
of Separation.

"In Christ's kingdom each one has equal right to judge for himself." ISAAC BACKUS

ISAAC BACKUS, born and raised an ordinary yeoman farmer in Norwich, Connecticut, in the second quarter of the eighteenth century, faced and wrestled with a fundamental question which has troubled Americans to this day—where to draw the line between the rights of individual conscience and the compulsory power of the State. This problem presented itself to him directly and personally in the area of religious conscience, and for fifty years he struggled to draw a line between Church and State different from that which prevailed in Puritan New England. In his career and in his writing he left a record of that fight which is still meaningful and relevant.

Born into a society which granted only bare toleration to a handful of dissenting sects, Backus began his life as a member of the established or Standing Order of New England—an order in which the Congregational churches had assumed the privileged position of an official State Church. Backus saw nothing wrong, at first, with requiring all citizens to pay taxes for the support of the Congregational churches and their ministers or to prove by written certificates that they were bona fide Baptists, Quakers, or Anglicans, no other sects being eligible for exemption.

After undergoing a profound conversion experience in the great religious revival of 1741, Backus suddenly found himself at odds with the Standing Church into which he had been baptized as an infant. Forced by his new religious convictions to break with that church for what he considered its spiritual and ecclesiastical corruption of Gospel Truth, he suddenly found himself outside the establishment—one of the despised dissenters of New England. When he became a Baptist he discovered how hard indeed was the lot of those who were merely tolerated. And, when he saw his brethren and members of his own family imprisoned, fined, and distrained of their goods for refusing to pay taxes for the support of a faith they believed to be erroneous, he began to fight to disestablish the Standing Order.

Though he fought for over sixty years, he died a quarter century before the victory he sought. For this reason his efforts have been forgotten or neglected by most historians. Yet his struggle was a revolution in the social and intellectual history of New England. Only a few radical nonconformists in his day believed that an orderly, moral, stable society could exist without a tax-supported established church. Backus and his brethren claimed that in the great religious awakening of the 1740's God had shed "New Light" on this question and that Christians were obliged to support this "new reformation" at the risk of their lives, liberty, and property, if need be.

Backus's fight to disestablish the Standing Order of New England was one of the opening battles of the American Revolution. The Standing Order frankly described it as "a rebellion against the STATE," just as the effort of the colonies to assert their rights in 1776 was considered a rebellion against the Empire. Backus's principle of voluntarism has prevailed, and his effort now seems part of the contest for the rights of individual freedom of conscience against the tyranny of the State. But the tension between the individual and the State is still with us.

In his life and writings Backus set forth the principles of separation of Church and State which were to predominate in American life until very recently. They were not, however, the same as those set forth by Jefferson and Madison in their more famous, but more quickly successful, fight to disestablish the Anglican Church in Virginia in 1785. Jefferson and Madison, operating from the rationalistic principles of deism or latitudinarianism, wanted to create a secular state with "a high wall of separation" to keep religion at bay. Jefferson, who viewed all religious creeds and sects as potential tyrannies over the mind of man, explicitly denied that America was or should be a Christian nation.

Backus and the Baptists wanted to separate Church and State in order to create a truly Christian state in which men rendered to Caesar only what was really Caesar's and devoted the bulk of their energy to serving God. Where Jefferson and Madison feared the machinations of the priestcraft and the "superstition" of orthodox Calvinism, Backus and the Baptists feared the persecution of the State and sought to keep the Christian churches free from the machinations of officialdom by insisting that since "Christ's kingdom is not of this world," His churches should be supported only by private voluntary gifts. Backus believed America was and ought to be a Christian nation, and he

looked forward to the day when it would be a Baptist nation. His was a pietistic version of the doctrine of separation, more like that of Roger Williams, with whom he
deserves to be compared, than like that of Jefferson and
Madison.

Jefferson and Madison were concerned primarily to protect the rights of man; Backus and the Baptists were concerned primarily to protect the rights of Christians—"the
essential rights of Christianity." "The church," as Backus
wrote in 1785, "is presented as a *chaste virgin to Christ;*
and to place her trust and love upon others, is *playing the
harlot,* and so the way to destroy all religion (Hosea ii:5)."

Throughout the nineteenth century the United States
Supreme Court adopted the position of Backus and maintained that America was a Christian nation, in fact, "a
Protestant nation." In the twentieth century the Court has
turned toward the more consistent, though secularistic, position of Jefferson and Madison. Today we are examining
again the meaning and purpose of this unique American
tradition to see whether it is still viable in a pluralistic
society. In the unending search for a usable line between
that which is Caesar's and that which is God's, it is helpful
and pertinent to understand the outlook of the man who
best exemplified the pietistic side of that tradition.

1

"The New Light" and the Old Tradition

". . . for much of what I have written I knew experimentally before I did doctrinally." ISAAC BACKUS, *Internal Call* (1754) p. x.

IN THE BEGINNING was the experience—the explosive, power-full, transforming experience of a direct confrontation with Divine Truth. The experience came to Isaac Backus, as it did to thousands of Americans, in the 1740's. The experience not only transformed their souls—infusing them with God's grace and thereby saving them from hell—but it recast their whole outlook on life. They had lived in a dark cave and suddenly the stone in front was rolled away. The blinding light of "the real world" shone in upon them for the first time. "The Lord God is a Sun," said Backus, and "when any Soul is brought to behold his Glories, them eternal rays of Light and Love Shine down particularly upon him to remove his darkness." *Particularly upon him,* let it be noted, and not upon all the world in general: "its Rays appear to point as directly to us as if there was not another Person in the World for it to shine upon." The Spirit of the Lord shone round about and, "coming with Power upon their Hearts," He made new men out of those whose souls He entered—new men ready to take over a New World.

The Americans who suddenly received this glorious "New Light" were transformed, and the influx of divine love or benevolence into their hearts moved them to transform others. No sooner did God let in the light and men begin to rush toward it, however, than many voices were raised saying, "No, no, it is a false light." These were the voices of Satan speaking through the mouths of a learned, established clergy too blind to see and through the aristocrats too entrenched in power to welcome change. To bring the New Light to the world it was necessary to fight against these forces—to revolutionize the false system by which they bound mankind in the chains of spiritual tyranny. To end spiritual tyranny so that the light of divine truth might shine clearly into each darkened soul called for a social and political revolution. *"My dear Fellow Men,"* said Backus in 1754, "Be intreated no longer to take Things by Tradition. . . ." This movement, which Backus and the Baptists called "the new reformation," historians have called the American Revolution. It began in the 1740's, and it ended almost a century later when the nation came of age.

Isaac Backus did not come from a radical background, but was born into the ruling elite of Connecticut. His father, Samuel Backus, was a well-to-do farmer in Norwich who served several terms in the General Assembly and would no doubt have risen even higher in public office had he not died unexpectedly in 1740. Isaac's grandfather, Joseph Backus, was a justice of the peace in the days when this office entitled a man to imprison, fine, whip, or send to the stock those who disturbed the peace; and Judge Backus did not hesitate to use this power against dissenters from the Standing Order. His great-grandfather, William Backus, Jr., was one of the early settlers of Norwich in

1660 and a proprietary founder of the neighboring town of Windham; as one of the legatees of the Indian sachem, Joshua Uncas, he received three shares of land of one thousand acres each, which were the basis of the family fortune. Isaac Backus's great-great-grandfather, William Backus, Sr., had come to Saybrook from England in 1638; "a smith or cutler" by trade, he became one of the original proprietors of the town of Norwich in 1659 and moved there with his family in 1660, shortly before his death.

Over the years the Backus family had inter-married with most of the leading families in the area—the Tracys, the Leffingwells, the Griswolds, the Edwards', the Huntingtons, the Caulkins, and the Trumbulls. Though the families were large, the accumulation of wealth and property was larger. Isaac Backus's grandfather had started a blacksmith shop in 1701 at the request of the town, which made him a grant of land for the purpose. When iron was discovered near the Yantic River in the town, the Backus family began an ironworks which eventually played a large part in supplying the naval and military hardware of the Revolution. In addition, the Backus family built and operated a sawmill, a gristmill, and a general store. The family farms were equally productive, as were their forests, their sheep herds, their orchards, and their cranberry bogs.

As became a family of wealth and importance, the Backuses were elected and appointed to their proper share of offices in the town and the colony. Many of them were selectmen; many (including two of Backus's brothers) served in the legislature; several held commissions in the state militia. After the founding of Yale in 1701, several Backuses sent their sons there. One of Backus's uncles became a prominent lawyer after graduation, and another entered the Standing ministry and married the sister of Jonathan Edwards. Backus's sister, Elizabeth, was the wife of one Revolutionary general and the mother of another. His cousin, Eunice Backus, was the wife of the second Governor Trumbull.

Backus's father did not go to Yale, however, nor did any of his brothers. His own education was limited to the local common or English schools which he attended in the winter and summer months when he could be spared from the farm. He grew up in a large house, considered a mansion in its day, and the family owned a slave and had an Indian girl apprenticed as a servant. Nevertheless Backus and his five brothers and five sisters did most of the chores.

Backus's mother, Elizabeth Tracy, had a greater influence upon him than his father. She too was from a prominent Norwich family. Her great-grandfather, Thomas Tracy, Sr., had been one of the original proprietors of the town; and on her mother's side she traced her lineage back to Josiah Winslow, Sr., the brother of Governor Edward Winslow of Plymouth Colony. Her brother Isaac was to serve in the Connecticut legislature in the 1750's. Backus always showed considerable pride in his family's ancestry and wrote a manuscript which traced its genealogy over five generations through both branches. His primary attachment to his mother, however, grew out of her religious influence upon him. In a memoir of her which he wrote after her death, he recalled that she "often mentioned to her children a work of conviction and conversion which she experienced about the year 1721." She had a second religious experience during the Great Awakening in 1741, soon after her husband's untimely death from measles. Isaac's conversion followed hard upon hers. Backus's father underwent a less emotional conversion in 1736 though Backus never mentions it; the family seems to have been neither more nor less religious than most of its neighbors.

Despite the fact that Norwich was a thriving town and

of some importance as a seaport, it was by no means a city. In 1730 it had a total of 171 freemen and in 1754 it had a population of 5540 souls, 223 of them Negro. Located fourteen miles up the Thames River from New London, thirty-eight miles by postroad east of Hartford and thirty-eight miles west of Providence, it achieved the distinction of being a half-shire town with New London in 1734. Twenty years later it was paying the highest taxes of any town in the colony.

In 1714, ten years before Isaac's birth, his grandfather, Joseph Backus, was temporarily expelled from his seat in the Connecticut legislature for leading a schism from the parish church in Norwich. Judge Backus and some of his friends had withdrawn because the church voted to adopt the ecclesiastical procedures of the Saybrook Platform, a system of church government drawn up in 1708 in Connecticut which seriously limited the independence of the parish churches to choose or depose their own ministers and to regulate their own internal affairs by a simple majority vote of the members. Judge Backus even went to Massachusetts Bay to seek the assistance of John Wise and Increase and Cotton Mather to prevent this perversion of the old congregational tradition. Ultimately the Norwich minister who had favored the Saybrook Platform was persuaded to leave the parish and a new minister, Benjamin Lord, agreed to revert to the older practices. Judge Backus and the schismatics returned to the fold, and life resumed its normal course in Norwich.

Benjamin Lord proved to be an able and popular pastor and Isaac Backus grew up under his preaching. Backus's parents joined the parish church in 1718, two years after their marriage, but they did not undergo a conversion experience prior to doing so. In the seventeenth century such a conversion had been essential to church membership since only the elect, those destined for heaven, were supposed to become members. But after 1662 many of the standing churches adopted a system known as the Halfway Covenant which allowed any person to join the parish church and sign the covenant or membership contract who professed belief in the doctrines of Calvinism and who lived an upright, moral life. Such persons were allowed only halfway into the church —they could have their children baptized but they could not take communion or vote in church affairs. This was the method practiced in the Norwich parish church under Benjamin Lord. It was always hoped that such halfway members would eventually undergo conversion and then, as in the case of Backus's parents, they were admitted to full membership.

Backus was born on January 9, 1723/24, the fourth child and second son. Baptized three days later, he grew up in a period of relative quiet in New England's history—the period of salutary neglect from the point of view of the mother country. The town had grown rapidly after 1690 and was a sizable seaport from which ships left regularly for Boston, New York, and the West Indies, as well as the British Isles. Nevertheless until he was over twenty-two Backus never traveled more than twenty miles from his home. His childhood was that of an ordinary New England farmboy. He spent long hours behind the plow, taking care of the cows, horses, and sheep, mowing the hay and rye, taking the corn to the mill, making cider in the fall, butchering pigs in the winter. He learned the rudiments of reading, writing, and arithmetic in the one-room schoolhouse, where he was taught by a variety of teachers, men and women, who passed through the community and were hired for a year or half a year by the parish's school committee. The Westminster Confession of Faith inculcated Calvinism along with the reading lessons in the school primer, and at least once a month the Rev. Ben-

jamin Lord came to the school to catechize the pupils. No
one in Backus's day separated the function of education
from that of religious indoctrination. Persons unlearned
in doctrine could be too easily led astray by "that old de-
luder," Satan. Calvinism taught that men were totally
depraved by Adam's original sin and if left to their own
devices would follow their selfish animal passions rather
than the laws of God. A learned ministry helped to show
them their moral and spiritual duties toward God, but
religious training and strict regulations by the laws of the
state were also essential to maintain the peace, piety, and
good order of the community. Government was an ordinance of God and it was the duty of the civil magistrate
to regulate the moral as well as civil life of the people for
the good of the commonwealth. The magistrates were also
to be "nursing fathers to the church," and hence to pass
laws for its support and to prevent disorderly or heretical
persons from interfering with the preaching of God's
truth. Civil magistrates could not, as the King and Parliament tried to do in England, appoint bishops or other
rulers over the churches; nor could they make laws to govern the creeds, ritual, or practices of the church. They
could, however, enforce the payment of religious taxes to
support religion. It was not until Backus was four years
old that New England became sufficiently tolerant to exempt Quakers, Baptists, and Anglicans from paying taxes
for the maintenance of the Puritan ministers and parish
churches (though these three sects had been free to worship as they pleased since the English Toleration Act of
1689).

As a child Backus attended the parish church regularly
with his parents. It was symptomatic of the carefully struc-
tured social order of the Bible Commonwealths of New
England that the meetinghouse seating was arranged according to wealth and social rank. Backus could measure

his standing in the community by the proximity of his family's pew to the pulpit. The Sunday morning service began at nine o'clock and the Rev. Mr. Lord, a graduate of Yale, wearing a powdered wig, black small clothes, and the Geneva bands, opened the service with a prayer which often lasted a full hour by the glass on his pulpit. When the last sands ran out he turned the glass over and began his sermon, which might last for two turns of the glass. After a psalm was sung, the congregation took a brief recess to eat cold lunches and then returned for a second sermon which lasted most of the afternoon. Conscientious persons often took notes as the minister expounded the Calvinistic intricacies of the complex and mysterious Word of God. In addition to Sabbath worship, the minister often conducted a mid-week service, and before the communion Sunday he also held a "preparation" service. Frequently throughout the year the governor proclaimed days of thanksgiving, fasting, or prayer when all work and recreation was forbidden and the parish attended services as on the Sabbath.

Despite the frequent admonitions of his mother and her recitals of her conversion experience, Backus took no particular interest in the state of his soul: "I lived a Car[e]less and Secure Life for more than 17 years," he wrote in his diary in 1751, "though in all this time I did never think that I was Converted but flatered my self with this that I would turn by and by" from sinful ways and receive God's grace.

Backus was physically strong and healthy. At maturity he reached almost six feet and though after middle-age he became stout, he was still solid and muscular. He always attributed his good health to his hardworking outdoor life as a yeoman farmer: "I was trained up to husbandry." He had dark hair and small, bright eyes. As an adolescent he was extremely bashful and scarcely opened his mouth. According to all the evidence he was obedient, introverted, and conscientious. His affection for his mother, and later for his wife and children, indicates a warmhearted and at times a sentimental nature which may have found his father's and grandfather's stern personalities too overbearing for comfort. Still the Backus family, like most New England families, was a tightly-knit clan whose unity sustained even the religious divisions brought by the Awakening.

The death of his father in November, 1740, precipitated a crisis. The mother too had been ill with measles, and she had a six-weeks-old child plus ten other children to care for. Though she was left financially secure, the shock of her husband's untimely death left her distraught. For six months she lingered in a state of depression, asking herself constantly why God had visited her with such a calamity.

Just at this moment the first wave of the Great Awakening broke over New England and the American colonies. George Whitefield, fresh from sensational successes as an evangelist in England, where he was associated with the outbreak of the Evangelical Revival, came to New England for his first visit in September of 1740. News of his success as a preacher had preceded him, and New England, already primed by the brief religious revival under Jonathan Edwards in Northampton in 1734-35, was tense with anticipation. Whitefield was a graduate of Oxford and ordained in the Church of England, but he was a Calvinist, and the Puritans had no qualms about hearing a good Anglican if he was also a good Calvinist.

Whitefield came through New England like a hurricane in the fall of 1740. Huge crowds gathered to hear him. He astounded them by the emotional fervor and melodramatic flourish of a kind of preaching which New Englanders had never heard before. The Puritans, distrusting the emotions, had always used a plain, severe style which even in the hands of Jonathan Edwards could hardly be called emotional. Whitefield raved and ranted, shouted and sang, wept and roared. The novelty of the experience literally bowled over the audience.

What he said was as shocking as the way he said it. He denounced the spiritual torpor of the people, blaming it partly upon their own lack of religious concern and partly upon the cold and formal preaching of unconverted ministers who "do not experimentally know Christ" because they had never experienced conversion and so could not preach it with intensity and fervor. Whitefield was not, of course, seeking to overthrow the established system in New England any more than in old England. He was trying only to revive it from within. His tour of New England lasted only six weeks, but it lighted a match to the dry spiritual straw which a host of other itinerant evangelists who followed him quickly fanned into a spiritual holocaust.

At the outset the religious fervor delighted the established ministers. Those who were able to imitate Whitefield's methods set to work to keep the enthusiasm going and were invited from one parish to another by ministers who were not so adept at this kind of preaching. The common people, who had never before found such excitement in religion, reveled in the experience. Many of them followed Whitefield from town to town, and when he left they urged their pastors to invite other preachers who were like Whitefield to preach in the parish church. The people of Norwich were no exception and Benjamin Lord was happy to oblige them. He believed that Whitefield's coming had produced "a great and glorious work of divine grace, and a great reformation of religion"—the Holy Spirit had come down and converted hundreds and thousands as a testimony to the fact that God was pleased with this new form of preaching.

Whitefield did not come through the town of Norwich, but everyone there knew of the religious excitement which he had stirred up. In the summer of 1741 Benjamin Lord, anxious to participate in the movement and obtain some spiritual blessings in his own parish, invited into his pulpit some of the most popular and successful imitators of Whitefield. "Mr. James Davenport came to Norwich," wrote Backus in his diary, in the beginning of August, "where he was met by Doctors Wheelock and Pomeroy, and meetings were held incessantly for three days. People were greatly affected and many hopefully converted." One of those greatly affected was "the widow Backus." The renewal of her religious faith pulled her out of her depression and elevated her into a state of spiritual exaltation. She now became one of the most fervent of the revival enthusiasts and her home became a center for prayer meetings and religious exhorting.

For the next two years the people of Norwich enthusiastically joined in the new spiritual fervor. A constant stream of revival preachers, some ordained and some not, poured through the town, travelling from place to place to keep the spiritual fires burning and gather the harvest of souls into the Kingdom. The outpouring of God's grace seemed miraculous and totally unmerited by the sinners to whom it came, yet they could not help but rejoice that God had entered their hearts, transformed their wicked souls, and elected them to eternal sainthood in heaven. So many were converted that people began to think that God must have some special purpose in view, some new dispensation for New England, perhaps even the millennial second coming of Christ. Jonathan Edwards, the most learned man of his day and the ardent admirer of Whitefield, speculated upon this possibility as almost everyone in his parish became converted and joined his church.

Isaac Backus, now seventeen years old, hoped to share in the blessings of the movement. His mother and many friends around him had undergone the great experience, and he was now convinced that he could not "put off my concern, as I had done before, for a more convenient season." "Now was the appointed time"; God had "now given me an opportunity to repent and turn to Him." If he neglected the opportunity, he "was lost for eternity. Time was then taken out of the way, and a vast eternity was directly before me, without any hope of ever having another day of grace, should this be neglected." So the visiting ministers had warned: now, while God was pouring forth his blessings upon all New England, the moment had come for Isaac Backus to awaken to his sense of his own sinful and lost state, to repent of his sins, and to turn to God and resign his will to Him.

At first he did not know how to do it. "For all the sound teaching with which I had been favored had given me no higher ideas than that a good disposition of mind was necessary in order to come to Christ for salvation." Benjamin Lord, like most parish ministers in the years prior to 1740, had preached a rather benevolent form of Calvinism—the old Covenant Theology which implied that if the sinner would do his duty toward God by living an upright, moral, pious life, God would eventually grant him salvation (in His own good time). But nothing Lord had said had shown Backus, or others in the community, how to bring about this glorious and all-important event. The preaching of Davenport, Wheelock, and Pomeroy had "awakened" him to a sense of his jeopardy. But "I felt like a stupid beast before God."

He went to Benjamin Lord, who said, "Be not discouraged, but see if God does not appear for your help." Later

Backus realized that this was absolutely the worst advice he could have been given. For upon hearing that God would soon come to help, "I was powerfully tempted to cast off my concern and to hope for help hereafter." In other words, his pastor, instead of pressing in upon him the dangers of his state and intensifying the urgency and concern which God had placed upon his soul, had endeavored to reassure him, to take away the sense of danger and conviction of guilt, to make him again "secure" and at ease in his conscience, leaving the ultimate resolution up to God. Fortunately Backus realized in time that this was the wrong approach. In fact, "this appeared plainly to come from the adversary"—from the Devil. God, or the Holy Spirit, caused him to put off his pastor's bad advice. His concern increased: "Powerful preaching and the sight of many in distress or joy, while I remained a hardened sinner, caused such anguish as words cannot express." Everyone around him was rejoicing and exalting. But he remained behind, left out, a sinner so apparently hardened and wicked as to be beyond redemption. "I grew worse and worse . . . I could find no good in me."

He made greater efforts to achieve salvation. But he was so ignorant of the proper manner of doing it, so badly instructed, that he could think only of going to more meetings and praying more fervently. Yet God had mercy upon him. "God laid open to me the plague of my own heart and the folly of seeking life [eternal life] by my own doings." He pointed out that "he was not obliged to have mercy upon me after all my doings." No one could force God to save him. The more a man strove to effect his own salvation the more he demonstrated his self-centered interest in his own well-being. Striving sinners were not seeking the glory of God. They were not resigned to accept God's will and humbly to acknowledge their own sinfulness and unworthiness. Instead they were confidently and self-justifyingly demanding that God take notice of their piety. Their primary motivation was the fear of hell, not the love of God.

God had mercy on Isaac Backus and forgave his presumption and the mistaken approach which the false or inadequate teaching and practices of the parish minister had encouraged. God "drew me off from all trust in myself or any creature, and led me to embrace salvation in His own way." The description which Backus wrote of his "new birth" is an almost classic formulation of the radically new morphology of conversion which underlay the pietistic spirit of his day:

As I was mowing alone in the field, August 24th, 1741, all my past life was opened plainly before me, and I saw clearly that it had been filled up with sin. I went and sat down in the shade of a tree, where my prayers and tears, my hearing of the Word of God and striving for a better heart, with all my other doings, were set before me in such a light that I perceived I could never make myself better, should I live ever so long. Divine justice appeared clear in my condemnation, and I saw that God had a right to do with me as he would. My soul yielded all into his hands, fell at His feet, and was silent and calm before Him. And while I sat there, I was enabled by divine light to see the perfect righteousness of Christ and the freeness and riches of His grace, with such clearness, that my soul was drawn forth to trust Him for salvation. And I wondered that others did not also come to Him who had enough for all. The Word of God and the promise of His grace appeared firmer than a rock, and I was astonished at my previous unbelief. My heavy burden was gone, tormenting fears were fled, and my joy was unspeakable.

What God enabled him to see by the divine light which shone in upon his soul was so new to him, "so different from my former ideas of conversion," that he could not at first believe what had happened to him. Then he heard a sermon which "gave the characters of the children of God, and I had an inward witness that those characters were wrought in me; such as a spirit of prayer, a hatred of sin, an overcoming of the world, love to the brethren, and love to enemies, and I concluded that I then had the sealings of the Spirit of God, that I was a child of His."

The "new light" and the "inward witness" were to become the keys of the movement which grew out of the Awakening. And when pitted against the "old light" of parish ministers like Benjamin Lord, they proved sufficiently powerful to alter permanently the traditions and practices of New England Puritanism. As a result of his conversion, Backus said, "new ideas and dispositions were given me." He became "a new man in Christ," a regenerated, born-again, converted Christian—one of the visible saints whom God had predestined for heaven. And "having experienced it," having felt the divine force as "a sensible experience" (to use his Lockean-Newtonian terminology), he could never be shaken from his faith in the validity, the reality, the truth and power of God: "the worship and service of God and obedience to His will were the delight of my soul. I found such happiness therein as I never had in all the vanities of the world."

At first the Rev. Benjamin Lord was delighted with the results of the revival. For twenty years his church had increased by an average of only five members a year. Now, suddenly, he was overwhelmed with new members. Thirty-two candidates asked for membership in 1741; forty-five in 1742; fifteen in 1743. And many of those "hopefully converted" or "awakened" or "under conviction," were momentarily expecting "the sealings of the Spirit of God" which would assure them that they too were among the elect. For these three years the parish was in that state of heightened spiritual awareness for which every Puritan minister yearned. His people were concerned for their souls, for the souls of their neighbors and their children; they hung on his words as never before, seeking more of the new light which had come to them under the preaching of itinerant evangelists.

However, by 1743, Mr. Lord began to notice that some people were carrying their fervor too far. Some itinerant revivalists were coming into his parish and preaching in private homes without his permission—and they were not learned ministers like Davenport, Wheelock, and Pomeroy, but merely ordinary men—farmers, coopers, cobblers— who claimed to have received an internal call from the Holy Spirit to become preachers. Such "illiterate exhort-ers" were so intent upon producing the outward effects of the conversion experience that they mistook "the ani-mal affections" for "the religious affections." That is, they worked upon the emotions of their hearers in order to make them cry, shout, groan, or fall fainting to the floor. They produced by a "mechanical" process what the Holy Spirit produced by a spiritual process. This was clearly the Devil's way to throw disgrace upon the blessing sent from heaven. Satan was using ignorant, misguided fanatics to delude the unstable and the uneducated people of the parish to think they had received the power of grace when they had not.

Backus noticed the same tendency: "This work [of God] was so powerful and people in general were so ig-norant, that they had little government of their passions. Many cried out and fell down in meetings." Backus him-self did not: "I had so much doctrinal knowledge that I never was overcome in that manner." Yet there was a dif-ference between Backus's criticism of this "crying out and falling down in distress" and that by Benjamin Lord and other opponents of the movement. Backus clearly implied that the emotionalism of the new lights was the genuine result of the powerful work of the Holy Spirit; he deplored only the fact that they were unable to govern their passions. Lord and the old lights claimed that there was absolutely none of the power of God in this kind of emotionalism.

In addition, some of the lay exhorters and their converts began to criticize Lord and the other parish preachers for their coldness, formality, and erroneous doctrines and practices: Their sermons were not "lively" and lacked the true spirit of the gospel because most of the ministers were not themselves converted. Experimental religion required that those who wished to demonstrate or lead others to the Truth must themselves have directly experienced it. The Standing ministers were also too concerned for their salaries; they catered primarily to the well-to-do and seldom paid pastoral calls on poor farmers on the outskirts of the parish; they put on airs, wore fine clothes and wigs, insisted upon flaunting their college degrees and being called "the Rev. Mr. Jones" or "the Rev. Dr. Jones"; they wrote out their sermons and filled them with literary flourishes above the heads of the common people; and they even wrote out their prayers instead of praying extemporaneously "as the Spirit moved them."

The parish ministers, on the other hand, had a long list of complaints against the New Light itinerant exhorters and their followers: through their ignorance they perverted the Scriptures; through their vanity they exalted themselves against faithful and learned ministers; they usurped the power of God in pretending to judge who were among the saved and who were not; they were rude, arrogant, boasting, and vituperative; they disrupted the peaceful harmony of the parish by holding boisterous meetings in private homes at all hours and turned the people against their lawfully chosen ministers. Among Benjamin Lord's parish records is an affidavit signed by several of his church members testifying against the

"Dreadful speeches of [an] open Enthusiast" named Nathaniel Lothrop, Jr. who came to Norwich to exhort on January 22, 1741/42. Lothrop said "it would be the pleasantis sight that ever my eyes saw if Christ would come in the cloud & take vengeance on all the workers of iniquity this night & to hear Christ give commission to the devils to drag your soul down to hell my dear sister Anne" —Sister Anne being one of his auditors who was apparently unimpressed with Lothrop's call to preach: "I challenge all the opposers [of my meetings]," said Lothrop, "to say that I have not got the Spirit of God in me for I know I have & I chalenge all men to call God to witness that I have not got the Spirit of God in me for I know (striking hard on his brest) that I have."

Many who had hitherto been favorable to the revival drew back in horror at such blasphemies. And Lord, fearing that his parish was fast getting out of control, began to use his Sunday morning services to denounce the false "lay preachers." In order to cool off the ardor of the New Lights he even refused to allow well known revivalists who were members of the established churches to return to Norwich to preach. To the New Lights these actions were further confirmation of Lord's own lack of religion and proof that he was opposing the work of God.

The lax prevailing practice in regard to admissions to church membership caused the greatest antipathy between the New and the Old Lights and eventually gave rise to the Separate-Baptist movement. The same "inward feeling" that made the New Lights who had experienced conversion conscious of their own salvation also informed them who were not among the elect. "The Saints," they said, "by Virtue of Grace in themselves, know the certainty of Grace in another." It became painfully obvious to them that many of those who had been admitted to church membership via the Halfway Covenant and a formal, written

account or their conversion were not "visible saints"—
persons who, to the visible eye of mortal man were among
the elect. Yet, as the New Lights pointed out, their Puritan forebears who founded New England had insisted
that no one should be admitted to full church membership
unless he had been truly converted. The Puritans had left
the Church of England and come to America precisely because they believed that it was contrary to the word of God
to permit the unconverted to enter the church, the mystical body of Christ. To sit down at the Lord's Supper
with persons who were sinners, reprobates, damned to
eternal hellfire, was to pollute and corrupt the whole
principle of a purified church. Slowly it began to dawn
upon the New Lights that perhaps the dreadful condition
of religion in New England from 1662 to 1740 had been
the result of this gradual "warping off" from the original
principles of their forefathers. The Awakening itself was
a call from God to return to the old ways, to purify the
church, to begin a "new reformation" in New England.

Backus saw this difficulty at once. And after his conversion in August, 1741, he debated for many months over
whether he could honestly join such a corrupt church and
take communion with worldly men who could not possibly
sense the holiness and spiritual meaning of that ordinance.
Yet the only way in which the church could purify itself
was by a majority vote of its members to rescind the practices of the Halfway Covenant and to adopt a more stringent method of admitting new members. And the only
way a majority could be obtained was for all of the new
converts to join the church and reform it from within.
After ten months of debate, he presented himself for membership on July 11, 1742, and was readily accepted. He
joined the church "concluding to bear those things as a
burden and to hope for a reformation." His conversion
had filled him with a longing to "enjoy the precious ordi-

nance of the supper" and he could not in conscience fore-
bear to exercise it.

From Benjamin Lord's point of view this spiritual conflict was unnecessary. According to Christ's parable of the
wheat and the tares the latter were not to be uprooted lest
much of the wheat be torn up too. Lord and the Standing
ministers took the parable to mean that the wheatfield
was the symbol of the church and that Christ was here
commanding that a charitable view was essential in regard
to church membership. For if men, with their fallible
judgment, were to try to distinguish between the saved
and the damned with too rigid or fanatical an urge
for perfect purity, they would ultimately uproot and excommunicate many who truly were saved but whose state
of grace was not visible to mortal eyes.

But the New Lights, like Backus, who entered the
church under the stimulus of recent conversion, began to
agitate for a return to the old practice. They interpreted
the parable of the wheat and the tares differently. To
them the wheatfield symbolized the world, not the church,
and Christ's command against uprooting the tares was a
command against persecuting dissenters who were outside the church. Christ clearly said that only those who believed in him on faith, who were therefore saved by grace,
should be members of his church. But He deplored any
attempt to impose conformity and uniformity upon the
world at large. The parable was directed therefore against
the Papacy for the Inquisition or the Anglican Church for
its persecution of Puritans and non-conformists, but it in
no way justified admitting non-believers, the unsaved,
into the church itself.

The Old Lights opposed any return to the old practice,
for once the church revoked the existing system of membership the next logical step would be for the New Lights
to excommunicate all those persons who had been ad-

mitted without being converted. And this would deny
them not only the right to take communion and to vote
in church affairs, but also the right to have their children
baptized. Though the Puritans did not believe that baptism of infants in any way contributed to their salvation,
still it was a comfort to a parent and a benefit to society to
have young children brought up under the watch and
care of the church. In a time when infant mortality rates
were exceedingly high, as they were throughout the colonial period in New England, few parents could deny themselves the solace, faint though it was, that their dead children had at least died within the covenant. Moreover, in
a corporate Christian society, religious training of the
young was a divinely appointed duty of the Church. This
was the difference between Christian civilization and
heathen barbarism.

It appears that when the New Lights in Norwich took
the first step in their new reformation and brought forward at a church meeting in February 1744/45 a proposal
to require that no one should thenceforth be admitted
to the church until he or she could give convincing oral
evidence of conversion, to be voted upon by the members,
the Old Lights refused to agree. Instead, the Old Light majority voted: "Though it is esteemed a desirable thing that
persons who come into full communion offer some public
relation of their experience; yet we do not judge nor
hold it as a term of communion." The New Lights, defeated in their effort to reform the parish church from
within, had no choice but to "come out" from its iniqui-
ties. In fact, some of them had already withdrawn from
the Norwich Church. They had waited four years for the
pastor and the church to see the error of their ways and to
heed the loud calls of God to reform themselves. Now
they could no longer compromise with their consciences
and with God's commands.

Led by some of the most prominent men and women in Norwich, including leading members of the Griswold, Caulkins, Backus, Hide, and Leffingwell families, the more radical New Lights walked out of the parish church and began holding meetings by themselves. Among these schismatics or "Separates," were Isaac Backus, his mother, and his uncle James. Later his brothers Samuel and Simon, his paternal grandmother, and his uncles Isaac and Hezekiah Tracy joined them. It was no light matter, for under the tightly-knit Church-State system of that day, separation from the parish church was a civil as well as a religious offense. All of the Separates were subject to fines, imprisonment, placing in the stocks, and possibly even whipping for their breach of the peace and their defiance of "the wholesome laws" of the corporate commonwealth. And ultimately many of the Norwich come-outers, including some of the Backus family, were imprisoned.

Anglicans, Quakers, and Baptists had won a grudging toleration (along with complete ostracism) in New England, but there was no toleration for obstinate, fanatical schismatics who claimed not to be a new sect but simply a more pure form of the established church. This was not a question of toleration but of revolution.

II

The Separate Movement and the Call to the Ministry

"Does not the core of all this difficulty lie in this, that common people [justly] claim as good a right to judge and act for themselves in matters of religion as civil rulers or the learned clergy?" ISAAC BACKUS, *Fish Caught* (1768) p. 114.

BACKUS DESCRIBED the origin of the separation from the Norwich parish church in these words: "The minister obtained a major vote in 1744, to admit members into the church without so much as a written account of any change of heart at all. At the same time he declared a strong attachment to the Saybrook Platform, which gave ministers power above the churches, and which his church renounced before they settled him. And by that power the ministers of Windham county, ordained a young minister in Canterbury against the vote of a large majority of the church there in the close of 1744. Therefore a large part of the first church in Norwich drew off from said minister, and met for worship in another place in the beginning of 1745."

The essence of the religious revolution which the Separate movement began (and the Baptists finished) lay in

church government and not in theology—though it became necessary eventually to modify Calvinism in order
that it might conform more nearly to the unforeseen ramifications of the new practices in church discipline and
polity. The major issues involved in church government
were the autonomy and purity of the church, the nature
of the ministry, and the relationship between Church and
State. The revolution came because the existing structure
and practice of the New England churches could not contain the new energy and outlook released by the experience of the revival. The challenge to individual parish
churches grew into a challenge to the associations or presbyteries which stood above them; when these proved unable to suppress or confine the new energies, the State itself
became involved in the disorder. For the Church and the
State were so intricately interwoven in the corporate
system of New England that a breakdown at the local level
ultimately compelled a realignment of the whole social
and political structure.

The Saybrook Platform assumed that every congregational church in the colony was subject to the regulation
of the ministerial association of the county in which it was
located. The county association, made up of all the established ministers (together with certain laymen chosen to
represent the churches in adjudicating some kinds of disputes) saw to it that only approved, licensed and ordained
ministers were settled over the parishes. It also had the
right to expel a minister from his church if he should, in
the view of the association, act contrary in word or deed
to the faith and practices embodied in the Platform and
the ecclesiastical laws of the colony. The state, in turn, was
obliged to support the judgments of the associations. It
could deny the right of a minister to preach and also to
collect his salary, even though he had a contract with the
town or parish.

This presbyterian or consociational system was in effect the ecclesiastical constitution of the colony. It was a far cry from the original congregational polity of the founding fathers and the Separates were perfectly correct in declaring that few of the founders would have approved of it.

When the Awakening began to get out of hand after 1742, the established ministers called upon the State to pass a law preventing itinerant evangelists from preaching in a parish without the permission of the parish minister. The legislature duly passed such a law under which many itinerants were punished, though local authorities by no means enforced it strictly. In 1743 the legislature also rescinded the Toleration Act of 1708 which allowed county courts to license dissenting churches whose members complied with the British Toleration Act of 1689; after 1743 only the legislature could do so. This effectively stifled several incipient Separate movements. In addition the legislature took disciplinary action against members of the Council and General Assembly known to sympathize with the New Lights—depriving them of their seats (as Judge Backus had been deprived in 1714) and depriving them too of their positions as Justices of the Peace and in the militia. Yale College, also a part of the establishment, expelled two of its students for attending New Light meetings and one for saying that a tutor "has no more grace than this chair."

The county ministerial associations likewise began to act. The New Haven Consociation in 1742 expelled the pastor of the established church in Branford for preaching to a group of Baptists and Separates against the wishes of the established minister in Wallingford. The Branford Church, controlled by New Lights, stood behind the pastor and voted to withdraw from the ecclesiastical system of the Saybrook Platform and return to the old Cambridge

Platform. The New Haven Consociation refused to countenance this withdrawal, and for his part in this action the pastor was deposed from his ministerial office. In addition, the consociation voted to "debar and suspend him from communion in any of the churches."

The two cases which provided the immediate stimulus to revolt occurred in Windham County in the towns of Canterbury and Plainfield, which bordered upon Norwich. Two of Backus's great-uncles were original proprietors of Canterbury and a large clan of Tracys, Leffingwells, and other relatives were intimately involved in the affair there. In 1743 the New Lights and the Old Lights in the parish church quarreled over the choice of a new pastor. The New Lights constituted the majority of the church but the Old Lights held a majority of the inhabitants of the parish. By ecclesiastical law both the church and the parish, voting separately, had to concur in the choice. But the Windham Consociation broke the law and declared the minority of Old Lights in the church to be the true church and then ordained the choice of this minority (concurred in by the Old Light majority of the parish voters) as official minister of the church and parish. The bitterness engendered by this action can still be felt in the venomous summary of it which Backus wrote forty years later: "thereby the first church in Canterbury was stripped of all legal privileges of a distinct religious society; and because they desired no new incorporation from the Assembly, but only petitioned to be exempted from supporting a teacher they never chose, their petition was disregarded, their goods were torn away, or their persons imprisoned therefor, for fifteen years; and the ministers who ordained him [the Old Lights] discovered no more compassion towards them than the priest and the Levite did to the man that fell among thieves. This is the plain truth without any exaggeration."

In 1744 Backus was eye-witness to an even more bitter struggle in Plainfield. Here the Consociation of Windham reversed the position it had taken in Canterbury and sided with a minority of Old Lights in the parish who concurred with a majority of Old Lights in the church to choose an Old Light minister over the objection of the majority of New Lights in the parish. The result was a separation led by Thomas Marsh, an aged and respectable deacon who was chosen by the Separates to be pastor of a new church. Marsh was arrested for preaching without a license and thrown in jail, where he remained for six months while the established ministers of the consociation did their best to suppress and intimidate the Separates.

These attempts at suppression merely stimulated the radical New Lights into more vehement opposition to the Standing Order. After 1745 a steady stream of separations began in one parish after another across New England. The grave threat to the stability and order of the system increased the conviction of the civil and religious authorities that the whole social order was being undermined. Ministers like Benjamin Lord, who had formerly been sympathetic to the Awakening, now drew back in horror. Lord's openly-voiced sympathy with the Windham Consociation ended any possibility of reconciliation with his own Separates, even though he never called upon the consociation or the civil authorities to put them down.

As many as thirty or forty radical New Lights in Norwich began meeting together for worship after January, 1744/45; eight years later the Separates and their sympathizers constituted a majority of the parish. Not all of those who joined the Separates in worship had been members of the parish church, nor were they only the poorer or unstable elements in the community. Some of the wealthiest men in the town separated; and while the bulk of the more respectable members stayed with the Standing

Order, the Separates had talented and influential leaders in every parish where they formed a church. Backus, being only twenty-one, and his mother, being a woman, were not among the outstanding figures in the Norwich group, though their presence lent it prestige. The real leadership came from Hugh Caulkins and Jedidiah Hide, from Joseph Griswold and William Lathrop, from Samuel Leffingwell and Backus's cousin John Leffingwell, Jr. All of these men had been members of the parish church, all belonged to leading families in the town, all were men of importance in the community.

At first the Separates met for worship each Sabbath at the home of Hugh Caulkins. Later they raised sufficient money to build their own meetinghouse on Bean Hill in the northwest corner of town not far from where the Backus family's blacksmith shop was located. Their meetings were filled with revivalistic fervor, and as "Elder" Hide preached under the power of the Holy Spirit the meetings often became scenes of pietistic ecstasy. Freed at last from the staid traditions and practices of the parish church, the Separates could give full vent to their feelings. Laymen, who in the parish church were allowed no part in the services other than as passive auditors, were encouraged in the Separate meetings to speak up if the Spirit moved them—to shout "Glory to God," or to testify to their own conversion, or to lead in prayer and even to exhort others to turn from their sins. God had spiritual "gifts" to bestow upon some of his chosen people—the gift of prayer, the gift of exhorting, the gift of preaching the word. And as the full meaning of "the new light" began to be understood, the Separates slowly realized that the common man who had himself directly experienced divine truth was equal to any learned minister in his ability to preach the gospel to the others, and superior to most of the learned clergy who had never been converted and therefore did not "know God." The congregation ceased to be "A silent democracy in the face of a speaking aristocracy." The Great Awakening gave this silent democracy its voice and the courage to speak up though the ancient and honorable upholders of tradition cried, "Havoc!"

On July 13, 1745, the Norwich Standing Church cited thirteen of its members (including Backus, his mother, his uncle James, Hide, Caulkins, Griswold, Lathrop, and Leffingwell) to appear before it and explain the reasons for their withdrawal from worship with them, thereby breaking the covenant they had signed when they became members of the church. These Separates appeared at a meeting of the parish church on August 28, and gave their reasons as follows: Jedidiah Hide said "The Church not making conversion a term of Communion," "The Gospel not preached here," and "better edification elsewhere." William Lathrop said he had separated because Mr. Lord was "Not a friend to lively preaching and Preachers, particularly not letting Mr. Jewett [a noted revivalist] preach once, and once forbidding Mr. Croswell [another ardent New Light]." Hugh Caulkins said "he was received into this Church when he was unconverted" and therefore was not properly a member nor were any others so admitted. John Leffingwell said that Mr. Lord was not "apt to teach" the Gospel. Samuel Leffingwell objected to "Mr. Lord's going from the [Cambridge] Platform." Joseph Griswold said he found "the Gospel better preached" elsewhere. "The Widow Elizabeth Backus said" only that her reasons for separating were "the same with others"; and Isaac, who had not yet found his tongue, said also that his reasons were "The same as the others."

Benjamin Lord, who carefully wrote down all of these comments in his records of the meeting, later summarized

the explanations given by the Separates under the following four headings, which constitute a fair analysis of the
basis of "the new reformation":

1. Neglect of Church Discipline, and Coldness and want of
application in [Lord's] Preaching.

2. The [gospel] Qualifications necessary for Church membership [were not adhered to in the parish church].

3. Private Brethren being debarred the privilege of Exhorta-
tion and Prayer.

4. The Laws of the State [i.e., the Saybrook Platform and
the laws prohibiting itinerancy and the licensing of Separate
churches].

The members of the parish church who remained with
Benjamin Lord (now by definition Old Lights though
some were moderate New Lights) then took these reasons
into consideration and, after deliberating, voted "that
their Reasons were not sufficient to justify their Separation
from the Church." On September 12, 1745, the Separates
were again called before the Old Lights in the church and
asked if they were ready to repent of their disorderly conduct and return to the fold. When they refused they were
"warned and admonished," and a month later the church
placed them under formal censure, an action which sus-
pended them from communion and all other church privileges until they sought forgiveness for their covenant-
breaking and were re-admitted. Having thus dealt with
thirteen leaders of the separation, the Old Lights then proceeded to take similar action against all of the others who
had separated. But the church never took the final step of
excommunication. Doubtless Benjamin Lord did not want
to make it too difficult for them eventually to come to
their senses and return.

After they had been denied their privileges in the parish
the Separates formally organized their own church on
July 16, 1746, using the same procedures that the found-

ing fathers of New England had originally followed. They heard and tested each other's oral relation of their conversion experiences and then signed a covenant agreeing to walk together in the way of the Lord as a church of visible saints. The members then chose Jedidiah Hide as their pastor and ordained him on October 30, 1747, with the help of a council of elders and brethren from the Separate churches of Canterbury, Plainfield, and Norwich Farms. Neither the civil authorities nor the Windham Consociation attempted to interfere.

The right of lay ordination was one of the most fundamental tenets of the Separate reformation. Majority rule in and by the church was essential. The Separates constantly harped on the theme that the established clergy were "lording it over" the brethren, the church members, by refusing to let the laity exercise their gifts and by exercising the right to veto the wishes of the majority. In many churches the voice of the congregation was reduced to a mere "yes" or "no" on propositions set before it by the pastor.

The right of ordaining their own pastors without the concurrence of a ministerial association or the license of the state was part of the democratic rebellion against the prevailing ecclesiastical constitution. "We are often represented as rebels," Backus later said, principally because they insisted that no one had a right to choose and ordain a pastor for a church except the brethren themselves. "In civil states," Backus wrote, "particular men are invested [as representatives] with authority to judge for the whole, but in Christ's kingdom each one has equal right to judge for himself." The Separates did not have to read John Locke's *Second Treatise on Government* to find the doctrine that "The people shall judge." They found it in the Bible and the Cambridge Platform. "The right of trying [testing and choosing] ministers which Christ gave to his church," said Backus, ". . . is now usurped by the clergy" under the presbyterian system of the Saybrook Platform. "They have thus robbed God's people of their right."

The brethren of any church also had the right to license anyone who had the gift of preaching and send him out as an itinerant. Two months after Jedidiah Hide was ordained, Isaac Backus himself felt a call to preach. It happened in the latter part of September after he had returned from attending the ordination of Solomon Paine and Thomas Stevens as pastors of the Separate churches in Canterbury and Plainfield. Suddenly "a conviction seized my mind that God had given me abilities that his church had a right to the use of, and that I could not withold it with a clear conscience." While he was still wondering whether this really was a call to preach, Backus was asked by Jedidiah Hide to go with him to the towns of Colchester and Lyme where a revival was in progress.

After participating in this revival, "I returned home with rejoicing and much life in my soul." Then, on September 27, while he was "alone in the woods," he had "such a converse with God as I never had before." And it became clear that "He called me to preach his gospel." But it was not an easy decision to make. As a layman, even though a Separate, he had a secure and comfortable future ahead of him in Norwich. He had inherited a good proportion of his father's lands and at his mother's death he would inherit more. The family enterprises needed his help and he had the ability to prosper in farming or business.

In his conversation with God in the woods, "I was lead [led] to count the cost as distinctly as ever I cast up any temporal sum." If he chose to become a Separate preacher it meant persecution, loss of prestige, living off the gifts of his auditors, and perhaps imprisonment. "Many and great enemies appeared in my way—reproaches, losses, imprisonment and death." In addition, he had doubts about his ability to preach. "My own ignorance and weakness" seemed so obvious: "I was slow of speech and very bashful."

But God answered him, "Cannot he who formed man's mouth make him to speak?" Still he doubted, putting up objections to each of God's replies until "it appeared to be trifling with Divine Majesty to attempt to make another objection. Therefore I was enabled there to give up my soul and body afresh to God, with all my interest, to go and serve him in preaching his gospel by his direction and assistance."

The Bean Hill Separate Church "allowed each brother free liberty to improve his gift in teaching," so the next day Backus asked permission of the church to test his gift by delivering a sermon. It was readily granted, for the pietists were always eager to see what new wonders God had in store: was this half-educated, bashful young farmboy perhaps destined to be a Moses to the beleaguered Separates? God "gave me a particular message, from the fifty third psalm, to lay open the universal corruption of mankind." It was a good Calvinist text, and as he began to expound it the Holy Spirit put the right words, or "the Word," into his mouth; he spoke "with special clearness," quite different from his usual slowness of speech. The sermon proved to be "to the acceptance of the church." He had put his "inward call" to the test and the experiment was a success. His brethren judged that God had indeed given him the gift of preaching and teaching.

The next day he went off again to preach itinerantly with Elder Hide. This time they traveled through Preston, Stonington, and Westerly, where they preached and "saw much of the power of the gospel upon the souls of men." He returned to Norwich on October 8, and later that month went on the road again, this time with his friend

John Fuller, a schoolteacher who had also recently received the call. After preaching with Fuller for two months he made another trip with Hide, this time clear across Rhode Island and into Rehoboth, Massachusetts where, he said later, "I first saw her who was since my wife, who had been converted the year before." But at that time Susanna Mason was just another New Light convert to him.

He continued to make preaching tours around eastern Connecticut, Rhode Island, and Massachusetts throughout the winter of 1746-47. Returning to his home in Norwich every two or three weeks, he soon found himself too restless to remain on the farm. For six months during the summer of 1747 he preached regularly to a group of Separates in nearby Windham. His friend John Fuller had now received a call to become pastor of a group of Separates in Lyme, and Backus evidently had hopes of being called as pastor to the Separates in Windham. "A few men there came out against me," he later wrote, "and some of them pretended to be perfect and immortal." Since he did not care to become associated with perfectionists and some of them evidently did not care for him, his hope of becoming a pastor there failed. It is significant, however, that for a time he had preached to a group which contained such radical, antinomian pietists; it is equally significant that he proved too conservative for them. Backus never did have any use for those extremists among the Separates who took literally the words of Jesus, "be ye perfect" and "whosoever liveth and believeth in me shall never die."

In June of 1747 Backus had taken a trip to Hartford, "where I saw mr. John Paine in prison for preaching the gospel without leave from parish ministers." But instead of making Backus fearful, the visit merely inspired him to continue his preaching. In December he began to read the journal of another New Light martyr, David Brainerd, who had been expelled from Yale for his piety. It "gave fresh animation to my mind," said Backus. And it also inspired him to begin a journal of his own, a diary which he was to keep faithfully for the next sixty years.

That same month a journey to the towns of Bridgewater and Middleborough, Massachusetts, decided his future career. His friend, Elder Joseph Snow, Jr. of the Second Congregational Church in Providence, a New Light who had led a schism in 1743, knew that there were some New Lights in Bridgewater who wanted to hear "lively" preaching; and he persuaded Backus to accompany him there. He may even have suggested to Backus the possibility of a pastorate there.

Backus arrived in Bridgewater on December 18, and the next day he wrote in his diary that the Christians in that town "appear'd to be really hungering after gospel food." And well they might have been, for they had been living for four years without a regular pastor. In 1743 these people in the southern part of Bridgewater had joined with a group living just across the Taunton River in the northern part of Middleborough to petition the General Assembly to set them off as a separate parish. Both towns were large and the meetinghouses were distant from these districts. The legislature granted their request, designated a boundary which united the southern end of Bridgewater and the northern end of Middleborough into an autonomous ecclesiastical corporation, and gave this new parish the name Titicut after the Christian Indians who inhabited the region and who had a church of their own there under an Indian pastor.

Under the terms of incorporation the inhabitants of Titicut were to proceed immediately to hire a minister and build a meetinghouse. But the Awakening had produced such tensions between Old Lights and New Lights in this area of Massachusetts that it proved impossible for the people of Titicut to obtain a minister. The majority of the people were decidedly New Light in sentiment, while the pastors of the churches to which they belonged were cool toward the Awakening and declined to give their members a dismission without assurance that the minister to be settled in Titicut would be acceptable to them. In addition, the first parish of Middleborough was already caught up in a violent schism between two factions, each of which claimed to be the true church and each of which hired and installed its own minister. For three years these two ministers conducted worship concurrently, each for his own adherents, while the matter was dragged through the courts and up to the General Assembly for final adjudication. In 1747 the General Assembly cut the knot by the unusual process of declaring both ministers legal and dividing the parish between them. While this dispute was going on in Middleborough it proved impossible for the people in Titicut to obtain support for the formation of their new church.

However, they had formed a parish committee which brought various preachers to conduct services for them on trial. The men they selected were all ardent New Light revivalists, like Solomon Reed, Silas Brett, John Wadsworth, Eliab Biram, and Daniel Whipple. But only two, Reed and Wadsworth, were college graduates. By tradition, and after 1760 by law, no man could be ordained as a Standing minister in Massachusetts without a college education or its equivalent. And while some exceptions to this rule were known, in the heightened feelings of the Awakening it seemed unlikely that any of the surrounding ministers (who were by law required to ordain new pastors) would have approved any of these men had the parish given them an invitation to settle. The inhabitants of Titicut themselves were undecided about the question of a learned as opposed to a converted ministry, though they all wanted lively preaching. In December, 1747,

Backus therefore walked into a situation ripe for Separatism.

He began preaching on December 18 in the homes of various people who knew and liked Joseph Snow. During the next ten days he delivered twenty sermons to attentive and eager audiences. The field, he wrote in his journal, was "white to harvest" newly awakened souls, and "my hart [heart] was so drawn forth towards God and in love to his People here that I felt willing to Impart not only the gospel to them But my own soul also, because they were made dear unto me, tho' I knew none of 'em personally." This feeling was reciprocated by many in the parish. A week before Backus arrived, on December 13, some of the more ardent New Lights had met together on the Sabbath and conducted some form of worship. On December 20, "Sundry of the Saints came and Besought me to tarry and preach here," he reported. This was only an informal invitation. But it was followed by a formal invitation by the parish committee on December 28. "This morning," he wrote, "the precinct [parish] Committee came to discourse with me, and Said they desir'd me to come and preach with 'em as a precinct minister, and Said they didn't doubt but I might be their minister if I wo'd be examin'd and come in regularly."

This was the beginning of a difficult decision for Backus and also of a serious misunderstanding. To Backus it seemed clear that the precinct committee was asking him to become the official Standing minister of Titicut Parish, despite the fact that they knew he was a Separate and did not have a college education. But how did the committee think that Backus could meet the legal requirement that he be an "able, orthodox, and learned" man? The precinct committee later claimed that Backus had deceived them and that they had not realized he was a Separate and under censure from his parish church in Nor-

wich. Backus may not have mentioned this fact, but it
seems unlikely that he purposely deceived them. Apparently at this time the Committee was sufficiently New
Light to try to stretch the law.

The response which Backus gave to the committee was
recorded in his journal: "I told 'em that I was clearly Convinced of duty in preaching to this people for the present
and I car'd not how many came to hear But I sho'dnt come
to preach to 'em under such notion as this that the precinct
instead of the Church had a right to lead in the Choice of a
minister: and as to being examin'd and coming in In an
orderly way, I told 'em if they were a mind to get any
neighbouring ministers to come and examine me, I was
free to preach to 'em or to give 'em the reasons of my hope
or of my practise. But then I sho'dnt leave it to man
whether I sho'd preach the gospel or no."

This seems more forthright than it was. While it frankly
stated his New Light belief that the church members and
not the parish should "take the lead" in calling a minister,
and his belief that the brethren and not the neighboring
ministers had the right of ordaining their own pastor, he
at the same time expressed no objection to "coming in In
an orderly way" by submitting to an examination by
the neighboring pastors as to his orthodoxy and his call
to preach; he also expressed his willingness to preach a
sermon for the approbation of this council of Standing
ministers. In short, he would submit to the forms but
wished to retain the substance.

Nothing appears to have been said by him or by the committee regarding his salary or how it was to be paid. The
fact that Backus did not expressly stipulate that he
would not accept his salary on the basis of religious taxes
laid upon the inhabitants of the parish may indicate that
he would have accepted such support. Compulsory re-

ligious taxes for the support of the ministry were not at
first an issue among the Separates.

One explanation for this official offer to Backus and
for his ambivalent reply may be that he and the committee
were aware of the recent installation of Silas Brett as the
Standing minister of the nearby town of Freetown. Brett,
though lacking any pretense at a college education or a
knowledge of Latin and Greek, had been officially approved and ordained by a council only three weeks before.
The circumstances were unusual—Freetown had long been
without a preacher and the neighboring ministers were
glad to see almost anyone of piety and good character installed over this reprobate community. Who could tell but
that this might be the shape of things to come, the beginning of the new reformation in Massachusetts, when a
converted ministry was acknowledged to be more important than a learned one?

However, Backus did report in his journal that his reply
to the committee "sem'd not very pleasing to 'em."
Nevertheless, before departing, the committee still said
"they wo'd have me preach to 'em for the present." The
interview thus resulted in his accepting an official invitation to supply the vacant parish temporarily, and he expected to be paid for this. In fact, he later complained
when he did not receive payment, though the money
would have come from religious taxes. Backus went to
work with a will: "We have had 24 meetings in 10 days,"
he wrote on December 29, "and [in] most of 'em the
Lord has appear'd very Wonderfully: many Backsliders
have been bro't near to God and abundantly refresh'd
with his Love and multitudes are struck under Conviction.
There is a great shaking among the dry bones. Glory!
glory to God alone!"

The twenty-three year old preacher was full of wonder

at what God was doing through his agency, and the possibility of becoming a member of the Standing ministry sorely tempted him. That an uneducated yeoman could attain this exalted rank and status and join the powerful ruling elite of Massachusetts was a prospect hard to resist. All he had to do was to yield a little to the official traditions and regulations of the state. "I found that fleshly Wisdom and a desire of the favour of men kept palling in my mind this lat[t]er end of the Week to have me let alone or abate the strictness (for the present) of some Truths concerning the Church of God that are most fit [fought] against in this Day; under a pretence of win[n]ing over a great number and so haveing advantage to do more good by and By." Like the apostle Paul, he was considering being all things to all men that he might win some to Christ. But being more of a pietist than Paul, he finally decided that this was a temptation of Satan which he must put behind him. He would not compromise.

Backus had another confrontation with the precinct committee on January 11, 1747/48. His revival meetings were causing a great stir; and the committee, made up of the most influential and conservative men of the parish, including Capt. Benjamin White, Esq., was fearful that matters might get out of hand. They did not care for some of the manifestations of the Spirit, the shouting, groaning, and falling down that occurred at the meetings; nor did they care for the arrogance of some of the new converts who claimed to be filled with the power of God: "I had a smart talk with some of the head men of this precinct," Backus wrote in his diary on January 11, "And they oppos'd the power of religion very smartly, but I was enabled with meekness and Boldness to stand for the Truth, So that they knew not what to say, but only at last they turn'd it off here that we must'nt look for such things now as the servants of God had formerly." What Backus considered laudable spiritual fervor, the committee members called extravagant enthusiasm based upon "inward feelings" and emotions. He later was to admit that "doubtless confidence has been carried beyond evidence in many instances" and that "I confess with shame that I have sometimes been thus ensnared." Apparently some of Backus's "saints" were claiming the spiritual power to tell the elect from the damned and had attacked the precinct committee and the neighboring ministers as tools of Satan and enemies of God for dragging their feet over Backus's installation.

Backus evidently felt it his duty to visit some of the Standing ministers in the vicinity. On January 15 he went to south Bridgewater to talk with the Rev. John Shaw, a graduate of Harvard and the Standing minister of that parish. "Many people gather'd in, and we had some close talk," Backus wrote. The talk was in the nature of a debate. Backus upheld the view that an internal call to preach was more important than classical learning: "I held that every true minister of Christ now had the same Call (as to the substance and Nature of it) as the prophets and Apostles had. . . . But he stood against it, and held that if men had College Learning, and were approbated and Ordained regularly (as he call'd it) They were ministers of Christ." Shaw went on to say that ministers who claimed to preach without learning and without a formal or regular approbation were "false teachers." But Backus answered that it was the unconverted ministers who were "false." He said he believed "that there were a great many [Standing ministers] in this generation that must come sooner or later to make that Confession and own that Man taught 'em from their youth and that God never Sent 'em. So we parted." If Backus had hoped to convince Shaw to approve of his installation in Titicut, he failed.

Finally, on February 2, Backus and his adherents de-

cided to take action themselves. For five years Titicut
parish had been without a church and without regular
services for worship. Now a revival was in full sway; the
new converts wanted a church, they wanted to be baptized
and take communion together, and for that they needed
a pastor. Whether the other parish ministers or the precinct committeemen agreed or not, the New Lights in Titicut were convinced that Backus had been sent by God to
help them. The revival he had aroused was proof that God
approved of this man.

Consequently, on that Tuesday morning, "the Saints
here first met to tell experiences in order to embody into
a Church." This preliminary meeting established which
of the recent converts were to form the nucleus of the
church. Backus then drew up a church covenant and articles of faith and practice for it. Two weeks later, on February 16, 1747/48, "The Church of Christ in the Joining
Borders of Bridgewater & Middleborough" was officially
formed. Sixteen persons, including Backus, signed the
church covenant, and within the next six weeks the church
admitted eighteen more persons. Ten months later it had
sixty-one members.

The articles which Backus drew up regarding doctrine
and faith were typical of the New Light churches, and as
expressions of orthodox Calvinist Christianity all of them
could have been accepted by any of the Standing churches.
Theology was not at issue. It was on issues of polity, discipline, and practice that the conflict arose. Basic to the conflict was the article stating "That Whosoever Presumes to
administer, or Pertake of the Seals of the Covenant of
Grace without Saveing faith are in Danger of Sealing their
own damnation. Therefore the doors of the Church should
be carefully kept at all times against such as cannot give
scriptural evidences of their union to Christ by faith." In
other words, there were to be no members admitted

into Backus's church under the Halfway Covenant or upon a mere written profession of faith. The articles went on to give the church the right to choose its ministers, deacons, and elders by a majority vote, and to dismiss them the same way, adding, however, that "it is convenient to advise with neighbouring churches of the same constitution" and to seek their advice on such important matters. The articles also repudiated the claim that the minister was in any respect superior in authority to the brethren: the pastor "hath no more power to Decide any case or controversy in the church than any private brother."

Backus had also made up his mind at last about the best method of ministerial support. Article Seven flatly stated "That the minister hath a right to a temporal maintainance from the people, & that it should be done by free contribution." In effect, of course, there was no other choice since only the incorporated parishes had the power to lay religious taxes. Upon the important doctrine of the priesthood of all believers and the right and the duty of the laity to exercise any ability they had to preach or pray in public, Backus wrote "That every saint is commanded to be faithfull to improve all the gifts & graces that are bestowed on them in their proper place & to their right end."

The radical pietists who separated from the Standing Order also wrote into the church covenant their belief in the doctrine of "further light," the faith that God had yet further light to shed upon his Word when the world was ready to accept it. The essence of pietistic revolution rested upon this doctrine. The Puritans used it to justify their revolt against the corruptions of the Church of England; the Baptists used it to break with the Puritans and later with the Separates; the Arminians, Methodists, and Unitarians used it to break with the Calvinists. And at the end of the nineteenth century, the social gospel and higher

critics used "progressive revelation" to break with the
evangelicals. The doctrine of "further light" insists that
all the institutions of Church and State be kept open to
receive new light as the occasion may demand or God may
will.

The original sixteen signers of the covenant Backus
drew up were Jonathan Woods, Joseph Harvey, William
Hooper, Ephraim Leach, Onesimus Campbell, Samuel
Alden, Joseph Phinney, Israel Washburn, James Hooper,
Joseph Harvey, Jr., Leah Washburn, Ruth Leach, Sarah
Leach, Esther Fobes, Abigail Fobes, and Abigail Fobes,
Jr. These ten men and six women, and those who later
joined them, were not as eminent as those who formed the
Separate Church in Norwich, for Titicut was hardly so
important a community. It was little more than a cross-
roads hamlet. But they were all respectable, hardworking,
and devout people. Most of the men were farmers.
Though they were ardent New Lights, none of them was
so ardent as to be a perfectionist or claim immortality.
By and large they were probably a fair cross section of
the community, distinguishable only by their religious
intensity. The Titicut area was probably settled by persons who had moved out from the older, settled areas in
search of cheaper land. Such people lacked the wealth,
power, and status that went with land in the older communities. In setting up an independent parish of their own
they sought some control over their own destiny, which
they lacked in the tightly knit, oligarchical structure of
the town centers.

Perhaps those who removed to these outlying areas were
outcast, resentful, or ingrown personalities who purposely
withdrew from the centers of power and conformity. Since
they probably found it difficult to walk to the parish
meetinghouse every Sabbath, and since the parish ministers were often remiss in making pastoral calls to more

remote areas, these people welcomed the warm attention of the itinerant revivalists preaching a lively gospel in their own vernacular and in their own homes. The revivalists in turn found such isolated hamlets to have "a wonderful hearing ear" and to be ripe for spiritual harvest. The New Lights preached a folk form of Calvinism and their preachers were the folk artists of their day. They brought the rarefied intellectualism of Puritanism down to the level of the common man. This was the contribution of the frontier to the development of the American pietistic temper—fervent, anti-intellectual, popular, egalitarian, but also often eccentric and flamboyant in its "wildfire" of enthusiasm. The New Light experimental rationale for Calvinism gave the common man knowledge through experience, and pietistic faith gave him the sublime confidence to trust his experience against the traditions, learning, and laws of his "betters."

Having formed a church in defiance of the authorities, the Titicut Separates also proceeded to call a pastor in defiance of them. The choice of course fell upon Backus. He had been told by the precinct committee shortly after he formed the church that he was no longer wanted to supply the parish ("They never offered me a farthing for my preaching two months at their request.") He was therefore a free agent. On March 31, the church held a meeting at Abiezer Edson's home and "all unitedly give in their Voice for me to be their pastor." He accepted. At the same meeting Jonathan Woods and Israel Washburn were chosen as deacons. The church wrote letters to the Separate churches in Norwich, Canterbury, and Attleborough as well as to that of Joseph Snow in Providence, asking them to send their pastors and lay messengers to assist in the ordination on April 13.

The formation of this radical New Light church aroused a storm among the more conservative people of Titicut.

It would now be more difficult than ever to persuade a good, college-educated minister to come. He would face a bitterly divided parish and endless quarrels and confusion. In fact it was not until 1756, when the Separate church broke up, that the parish was able to obtain such a minister.

The opposition to Backus was often scurrilous: "I had many things thrown upon me to represent my Carecter odious and to hinder me in this glorious Work. Sometimes the World wo'd tell that I had a Wife and 2 or 3 children up in the Country: at other times they wou'd say that I had Bastards in this or that place. And when I went a Journey to see my friends in the Summer, some Boldly asserted that there was a girl or two with Child by me here so that I wo'd never dare to come back again." Backus reacted to these slanders in true pietistic fashion: "But none of these things mov'd me, knowing that I had a clear Conscience before God."

On the day of his ordination a large crowd assembled in Bridgewater outside Joshua Fobes's house, where Backus had taken up residence and where he often held church meetings. Elder Jedidiah Hide from the Bean Hill Church was present, as well as Backus's brother Samuel and another lay member of that church, William Lathrop. Elder Solomon Paine came from the Separate Church in Canterbury and brought as a lay messenger Ebenezer Cleaveland, one of two brothers expelled from Yale in 1744 for attending Separate meetings. Joseph Snow from Providence and Elder William Carpenter, whom Backus had seen ordained over the Separate church in Attleborough four months earlier, were there. "Br. Hide brought a letter of Recommendation for me from the [Separate] Church at Norwich that I belong'd to before and this Church [Titicut Separate] did now openly manifest that they receiv'd me into their felloship."

Just as the ordination was about to begin "Benjamin White, Esq. one of the Committee of this Precinct rode up among the throng of people and spoke out aloud and Said that in the Name of the Committee of this precinct he Forbid our proceedings." There was a momentary silence as the crowd waited to see whether White had brought constables with him to arrest Backus. "Some others rose in open opposition" to the proceedings. But when no constables appeared it "caus'd the Saints to cry to Heaven for mercy on 'em" that opposed us and "stur'd up their Souls to come near to God." The assembled elders decided to proceed in spite of White's order and the heckling of their opposers. As Elder Snow began to preach the ordination sermon preceding Backus's installation, "Several neighbouring ministers rid up and Sat" on their horses watching the proceedings ominously. These were the Rev. John Angier and the Rev. John Shaw, ministers of the first and second parishes in Bridgewater, and the Rev. John Wales of the nearby town of Raynham. Their presence quieted the crowd again, but they "said nothing openly" and the ceremony continued.

"When Brother Snow had done I went on and gave a Particular account of my Conversion, then of my Call to preach, and Lastly of my Call to take Charge of this People. . . . and I did solemnly then in the presence of God and before that great Assembly give up my Body and Soul and my all to the Lord and to this Church. . . . And the Church did openly manifest That they did Receive me as a gift from God to go on with 'em in this solemn Work." The Separate elders declared "that we were join'd together as pastor and flock" and "they desir'd that one of the Church might assist in Laying on of hands (as is usual among us) for an open token that the Power of Ordination is in the Church." After Solomon Paine delivered a sermon to conclude the ceremony the crowd dispersed.

The next morning at a meeting of the church "Considerable Confusion" arose when some of the members, a bit overwrought by the occasion, declared that the Spirit had pointed out to them that this or that person should be deacon and this or that person was "Call'd to preach the Gospel." Backus said "Their declarations were Chiefly from wrong and false notions and Imaginations" and he managed to calm them down. Jonathan Woods and Israel Washburn had already been chosen deacons and Backus wanted to proceed to ordain them as such. "But they Sem'd to hold Back," and said that they would "Wait for clearer Light" before accepting ordination. The church then voted to admit Phoebe Leach as a member, and since she had never been baptized Backus performed that rite by sprinkling.

That night James Keith, one of the leading men of the parish, at whose home in Bridgewater Backus had often held meetings, "came in and forbade me preaching any more at his house." Keith, who would have accepted Backus as the official minister of the parish, balked at the forming of a Separate church. "I told him," said Backus, "that I didn't want at all to Crowd upon him Conterary to his mind, but he must take heed what he did in shutting the gospel out of his house. Afterwards I felt a sweet peace in my mind and a resting on God. Glory to his Name."

For the next month Backus continued to preach at private homes in Titicut, holding regular meetings for Sabbath worship at Joshua Fobes's house where he boarded. A spirit of revival continued in the area and new conversions brought new members to the church. On May 8 Backus performed his first communion service "and 'twas the most glorious season that ever I had in pertakeing of it in my Life." He also noted in his diary that it was now five months and five days since he had arrived from Norwich, and during this time he had preached 109 sermons in Titicut and seen "about a dozen Souls Converted."

Life moved with deceptive smoothness over the next ten months. In June Backus took a trip back home to Norwich and in September "my dear Mother came here, and staied about a fortnight, and on Sept. 26, I set away and went with her to Norwich." But in November he and his church members at last came face to face with the hard realities of the ecclesiastical laws of Massachusetts. Backus himself faced imprisonment; and that gave a whole new turn not only to the life of his church but, as it turned out, to his career as a minister.

On March 31, 1747/48, the very same day on which he had been called as pastor by the Separates, the rest of the parish had held a meeting to lay a tax of five hundred pounds for the completion of the meetinghouse. As the law prescribed, the assessors then proceeded to lay this tax proportionately upon all the inhabitants of Titicut in proportion to their property and polls. Backus was assessed five pounds to build a meetinghouse in which he would never worship. His members were similarly assessed. There being no Baptists, Quakers, or Anglicans in the parish, no one was exempted from these religious taxes. Refusal to pay meant either that the tax collector could take a man's horse, cow, saddle, or other property and sell it at auction to pay the tax, or that he could seize the body of the delinquent and place him in jail.

On November 21, 1748, with the tax collectors due at any moment, Backus's church wrote a letter to the inhabitants of Titicut parish protesting against their being taxed. It pointed out that when Backus had first come to Titicut the parish had officially invited him to preach and had then later withdrawn from attending his services. Those who had found his preaching acceptable and continued to hear him regretted this division, but they said they were willing to arrive at some compromise. "We would propose, that if you will again return and Joyn with us In meeting &c: you are hertily welcome, Shall be freely Excluded from all Charges heretofore Created in the Setteling our minister and we are ready freely to Joyn in Compleeting the meeting house to go on in love together Even till Death Shall Part." In short, they asked that Backus be accepted as the parish minister on New Light terms. "But if this is So mean you Canot Conseed to it, We would propose to go on in peace though we are not agreed to walk together. Intreating you would not Press upon us to help to build you a meetinghouse & maintain a minister when we ask no Such thing of you." That is, they asked to be exempt from religious taxes. "You will own that oppression will make a wise man mad, and much more Such as we are; & pray Consider would you Like it; if we were a few more in number than you to be forced to help us build a meetinghouse and maintain our minister? we Doubt it much. & yet we all talk of Giveing Liberty of Concience freely and if So: pray where's the Golden rule?" Technically, of course, if the Separates were a majority they would control the parish; but it was improbable that the courts would uphold any taxes they might lay for the support of an unauthorized minister like Backus.

To this letter the parish sent an answer signed by the parish committee, Benjamin White, Esq., Robert Washburn, Amos Keith, and James Keith. This letter spelled out exactly those elements in the prevailing system against which the radical New Lights were rebelling. It began by saying "we very much Disapprove of him who you call your minister, one Mr. Isaack Backas, as being

won [one] who is in no measure fit to sustain the ministerial office." He was under censure from the Norwich
parish church; he had deceived the parish committee when
he first came to Titicut; he had no regular call to preach
but simply claimed an "Extraordinary Call" similar to
"that of the prophets and apossles. . . . So by this
means Raising an high opinion of him self in the
thoughts and Sentiments of the more Ignorant"; he had
a strange "notion" about the ability of "True Believers"
to know who are and are not among the saved; he was erroneous in doctrine; and finally, "he goes about from place
to place as a preacher to the hurt and prejudice of Religion and to the Disturbance of the Peace" among the
"well Constituted Churches of Christ" in this area.

Having proved that Backus was not a fit man to be
the parish minister, the committee then went on to prove
that it would be wrong to exempt him and his followers
from religious taxes. In the first place, they were practic-
ing religion "in a bad Cause and in a sinfull way and
upon a false foundation." It was therefore necessary "to
break it for your good." To allow them to continue unhindered "wherein you are wrong and out of the way of
Truth . . . would be to purchase peace at the Expence
of Duty." In the second place the committee reminded
the Separates that they had been among those who had
petitioned the General Assembly in 1743 to be set off as a
parish and they were obliged to abide by the terms of
the incorporation of the parish; it was both their moral
and legal duty to help build a meetinghouse and to install
and support a legally qualified minister. "Is it our sin that
we urge and press you to Do your Duty . . . when we
urge and press you to go and Joyn with us in Calling an
settling a pious and Learned ministry among us . . . Tis
to do that which is Required at your hands both by God
and the Christian magistrates. . . . Shal we Let you

alone in the Neglect of your Duty to the Emenent hazard
of your own spiritual intrist and the intrist of your Children after you: and although we live in a Christian government must we be silent and never make use of the power
and authority of the Christian magistrate to Reclaim and
Reform you: is this oppression, is this going Contrary to
the Golden Rule, Does this infringe upon the Liberty of
Conscience which God gives, is this persicution?"

The committee answered its own rhetorical question
and in doing so it spelled out the basis of the argument
over the separation of Church and State with which
Backus had to wrestle for the rest of his life. Oppression
"can't mean and intend that Tis unwarrantable or sinfull
for men to urge and press others to a complyance with their
Duty as it is pointed out by the Laws of God or the good
and wholesome Laws of the Land and in case men through
obstinacy and willfulness [refuse] and so will not make
good their Lawfull Contracts [&] Covenants the original
good and Design of their being incorporated into Distinct
[religious] societyes [or parishes] and so Tis no oppres-
tion. . . ." Under the Golden Rule the committee said
it would want their neighbors to force *them* to do their
duty if *they* were in error. "Liberty of Conscience according to the word of god is not for men to Live as they list
or Do as they please while they maintain Erors in Judgment, Disown the truth of god, Exclaim against a faithful
ministry, make Light of that good order and government
which Jesus Christ has set up in his church; neither does
God himself countinance or give Liberty to any men to
follow the Dictates of a missguided Eronius Conscience. . . ." "Let it be observed that there is a great difference between persecution and prosicution."

Three-quarters of a century were to pass and Backus
was to be in his grave before the people of Massachusetts
yielded to the radical New Light view that the state should

indeed allow individuals to "act and Conduct as they pleas" in matters of religion even if it meant imperiling their souls, the destruction of the parish system, the end of compulsory religious taxation, and the abandonment of the Puritan ideal of a corporate Christian commonwealth.

Having failed to win a compromise, the Separates could now only wait for the tax collector to knock at their doors. When he did, some of them yielded to necessity and paid. Others heeded their consciences and watched the collector take their goods and sell them at auction. And some were taken to jail.

On February 6, 1748/49 the constable came for Backus himself: "This morning I was Seaz'd by the officer," he wrote in his diary. "And he thretned to Carry me to Prison for the precinct rate but glory to god he gave me a Sweet Calmness and Serenity of Soul—not to fear him nor to treat him with any bitterness. I told him that they were going on in an unscriptural way to Support the Gospel and therefore I could not do any thing to Countenance them in Such a way. He told me if I would not pay him he would imediately Carry me to Jail. But just as he was going to drag me away there Came a man and Called him out and paid him the money So that he was forced to let me go. Lord may this trial be blest for my Eternal good."

The man who paid his tax was Captain Edson, one of the prominent men in the parish at whose home the Separate Church had been formed. Edson, however, had withdrawn from the group and was now among the conservatives in the parish majority. His help to Backus may have been motivated by friendship or out of personal distaste for this kind of action. It was not out of sympathy for Backus's cause.

Other members of Backus's congregation were not so fortunate. One woman, Esther White, was sent to Plymouth jail for refusing to pay a tax of nine pence to support

the minister in Raynham where she lived. She remained
there for a year, refusing to let anyone pay her tax for her.
Backus paid her several visits at the jail where they prayed
together. "She told me," he said, "that the first night she
was in there she lay on the naked floor, and she said that
she never imagined that the floor was so easy to lie upon
before . . . and she said that she was easy to stay there
as long as God saw best she should."

One of the Separates then discovered that there had been
a technical flaw in the action taken by Titicut Parish
in laying the tax. The notice calling the parish meeting
which voted the tax had been issued over the signature of
the precinct committee instead of being posted by the
constable at the order of the committee as the law required. Legally this invalidated the meeting and therefore the tax itself. One of the Separates whose goods were
taken for his tax brought suit against the assessors for
trespass on the basis of this technicality. The lower court
upheld his claim but the parish then appealed to the Superior Court. At the same time the parish also petitioned
the General Court to validate their meeting and the tax
despite the acknowledged flaw. The legislature granted
the petition and the Superior Court thereupon sustained
the appeal of the parish against the lower court's decision.
As soon, therefore, as the parish could find a qualified
minister ready to settle as their pastor, the Separates would
face new taxes to pay his salary.

Two months after his own near-imprisonment, Backus
decided to make a general appeal to the General Assembly
on behalf of all the Separates in the colony. On April 18,
1749, he wrote letters to the Separate churches which had
sprung up in Attleborough, Norton, and Rehoboth, requesting them to attend a special conference in Attleborough on May 24, for the purpose of drawing up a
petition to the General Court requesting exemption from

religious taxation. Separates everywhere, whether they had formed a church and installed a pastor, as in these four towns, or whether they had merely come out from the parish church and worshipped privately under a lay exhorter, faced the same problem as Backus and his congregation. They now began to think of themselves as a united body, a denomination.

Backus summoned them to "go to our rulers, as Moses did to Pharoh, to ask them to Let the People go." The Separates found a legal basis for the claim to tax exemption in the Charter of 1691, still the fundamental law of the colony or province, which granted "liberty of conscience . . . to all (except Papists)." It was under this clause that the Baptists, Quakers, and Anglicans had obtained their special laws exempting them from religious taxes. If these dissenters, who differed far more radically from the Standing churches, were exempt from religious taxes, why should not the Separates be?

The letter went on to say that the plan was "to Draw up a Petition to Send to our general Court to let them know what we hold [as our principles] & desire them to give us that liberty that the word of god gives us & that our King allows us and so that if they won't hear us that we may Send to England." Having drawn up this petition, the plan was then "to send it to the rest of the [Separate] Chhs. in this Province that we might all act in fellowship together in these things. . . ."

The Separates did meet in Attleborough and drew up a petition. They decided to send "copyes around to the Saints in various parts of the government," said Backus, "and it fell to my lot to Carry a Copy down to the Cape." He arrived there on May 29, and "The next day I visited 3 Harwich Bretherin in Barnstable prison for rates." They signed the petition. He then went to Harwich where he preached and asked for more signers. "Out of Harwich," he reported, "Chattham and yarmouth there was 36 that Sign'd it and they gave £4 18s 1d for to Carry on the affair." He returned to Titicut where he obtained 66 more signatures and an additional £11.16.10 from the Separates there and in Raynham.

The petition was presented to the General Assembly by Samuel Peck and John Paine of Rehoboth on June 7, 1749. It had a total of 184 signers "Many of Whom are Free men." It began by saying that "God has given to every Man an Unalienable Right in Matters of His Worship to act for himself as his Consciance reseves ye Rule from God." After mentioning "our fore Fathers who left their Pleasant Native Land for an houlling Wilderness of Savage Men and Beasts that they might have Liberty of Consciance" it went on to quote the charter. It protested against those "Ecclesiastical Laws" which "Imprison Some and put some in ye stock[s] and also take away some of our Goods and Chattles to maintaine" ministers whom they could not in conscience listen to. And it concluded by asking the legislature to enact "Universal Liberty" or at least to forbid "ye Execution of sd Ecclesiasticall laws." It was the first of many scores of petitions on this subject in which Isaac Backus was to have a hand over the next half century.

The petition was discussed first in the lower house and "After Conciderable Contention upon it, they Chose a Committee to Conferr upon it and so sent it up to the Council" or upper house. The upper house refused to concur with the decision to appoint a committee of investigation "so there was nothing further acted upon it."

While Backus was debating whether to carry the petition on to the King, a crisis arose within his church which put everything else out of his mind. It was the beginning of a crucial alteration in the New Light movement which within a few years not only wrecked Backus's church but destroyed the burgeoning Separate denomination as well.

III

The Separate-Baptist Movement

". . . as none are the proper subject of baptism but real saints, so every such soul ought to be baptized by immersion before they come to the Lords Supper." Isaac Backus, "Diary," (1756).

THE GREAT CRISIS in Backus's church grew directly out of the anxieties relating to religious taxes. On August 7, 1749, "two brethren of our church brought a dispute into it against infant baptism and one of them declared that he believed that God had opened up a way for our deliverance from bondage by becoming baptists. This raised great heats and debates." Backus said of the claim that God wanted the Separates to become Baptists so that they could obtain the legal privileges of exemption from religious taxes, "This raised great fears in my mind that these [antipedobaptist] principles were wrong."

Yet it was a mistake to assert, as contemporary opponents did, that the Separate-Baptists were motivated primarily by the desire to escape taxes. This was totally out of character with the pietistic temper. Quite apart from the tax issue, antipedobaptism was a logical development from the radical New Light principles of the Separates. In fact, the Separate movement was a bridge from the Puritan to the Baptist or evangelical movement which grew out of it.

Backus himself was later to produce many polemical tracts, as well as a four-volume history of the Baptists in New England, to prove that antipedobaptism was the logical outgrowth of the New Light of the Great Awakening. Yet when this issue first arose in his church, Backus fought vigorously against it.

To begin with, Backus, like most Separates, clearly shared the accumulated religious and social prejudice the Puritans had brought from England against the Baptist views. The Anabaptist movement had nearly wrecked the Reformation in Germany in the early sixteenth century, and the heresies and madness of Münster in 1534-35 had given these doctrines a name so black that two centuries had not lightened it. The Puritans insisted that all subsequent Baptists would sooner or later come to the same position. A Massachusetts law of the 1640's vividly summarized the prevailing attitude towards them:

Forasmuch as experience hath plentifully and often proved that since the first rising of the Anabaptists about a hundred years since they have been the incendiaries of the commonwealths and the infectors of persons in main matters of religion and the troublers of churches in all places where they have been, and that they who have held the baptizing of infants unlawful have usually held other errors or heresies together therewith though they have (as hereticks use to do) concealed the same till they spied out a fit advantage and opportunity to vent them . . . which opinions, if they should be connived at by us, are like to be increased amongst us, and so must necessarily bring guilt upon us, infection and trouble to the churches, and hazard to the whole commonwealth.

This law therefore banished them from the colony, and any who wandered back into Massachusetts were imprisoned, fined, and whipped. Even toward the end of the seventeenth century, when a Baptist church had been founded in Swansea and another reluctantly tolerated in Boston itself, their views were still judged a threat to the safety and good order of society. As one Puritan put it,

theyr very principle of makeing infant Baptisme a nullity, it doth make at once all our churches & our religious, Civill state & polity, & all the officers & members thereof to be unbaptized & to bee no Christians & so our churches to bee no churches & so we have no regular freemen, which by our laws are to bee members of churches; & so we have no regular power to choose Deputies for any Generall Courts, nor to chuse any Magistreates; but all being, according to that pernicious doctrine, non members of any true church, and all our holsom lawes & orders made a nullity & that hedge is pulled downe & all left open to state destroyers . . . so that our very fundaments of civil & scared order, here in New England, are at once thereby . . . overturned.

To deny that God required the baptism of infants was to subvert the whole structure of the Bible Commonwealth.

The laws exempting Baptists from taxes, forced upon New England from the home country after 1728, merely exacerbated the prejudice against them. Now jealousy and anger over their privileged position was added to disdain for their heresy and fear of their subversion. Any increase in the number of Baptists in a town or parish meant an increase in the size of the religious taxes which the other members of the community had to pay to support the established church and minister. It was not long before any man converted to Baptist views was accused of being a "tax-dodger." News of an immersion (to wash away one's sins) was soon greeted with the popular jibe, "Ah, neighbor Smith, I hear you have been dipped to wash away your taxes."

The problem was not serious so long as the Baptists remained social outcasts. It was hardly worth the stigma of becoming a Baptist just to save a few shillings; the social penalties were too great. But the pietistic mood of the Great Awakening put the problem in a completely new light. The experiential knowledge of being "in the Truth" became a sufficiently powerful stimulus to make social martyrdom bearable and even honorable. A Separate who had already borne the scorn of ostracism for withdrawing from the Standing Order had little more to lose by becoming a Baptist and (tax exemption aside) he had everything to gain by following the new light God had given him wherever it might lead. For many pietists the Baptist position even seemed attractive because of the contumely heaped upon it.

Consequently, when many Separates began, after 1749, to believe that that "further light" was opening to justify the antipedobaptist position, the Puritan system faced a crisis of considerable proportions. There were thousands of Separates scattered through almost every town in New England, and in some parishes they constituted a majority of the inhabitants. How could the parish system sustain itself if all of these suddenly transferred their pietistic fervor to the Baptist cause and became tax exempt?

Fortunately for the Puritan system, the prejudice against the Baptists was sufficiently instilled among the Separates and their pietism was sufficiently impregnated with the conservative theology of Puritanism to prevent such a mass transference. Instead the debate over infant baptism split the radical pietists, turned their energies inward against themselves, and blunted their thrust against the Standing Order.

In this new movement, Isaac Backus became the leading figure, and his shift from the Separate to the Baptist camp is central to the religious history of New England in these years. Like most Separates, he was raised in the Standing Order and imbibed all of its anti-Baptist prejudices. Nevertheless, as he examined the question which his brethren, Ebenezer Hinds and Jonathan Woods, forced upon him in August, 1749, he discovered that the Baptist position resolved so many of the inherent contradictions in the Separate position that he at last became convinced that God was indeed shedding further light upon His Word and revealing the correctness of the antipedobaptist position, hidden so long in darkness by the corrupt teaching and practice of the Puritan tradition.

Setting out to refute Hinds and Woods, Backus turned first to the Bible, the complete and perfect Word of Truth. To his suprise he now found that the texts which he had formerly considered as indisputable proof of the necessity for infant baptism were ambiguous and uncertain. He could find no clear and express command for the baptism of infants. Nor could he find any example for infant baptism, though the Puritans had insisted that since the apostles baptized several whole families there must have been children among them. The words of Jesus in Mark 10:14 and Luke 18:16, "Suffer little children to come unto me for of such is the kingdom of heaven," seemed no proof either way.

Next he examined the claims of Baptist scholars in England that infant baptism was a corruption brought into the Christian church in the second or third century. To the anti-institutional mind of the pietist, it seemed logical to assume that this corruption had been given the sanction of canon law by priests and rulers anxious to cement their superstitious control over the common people. Even the Puritans agreed that the Roman Catholic doctrine that infant baptism served for the remission of original sin was corrupt. What function then did infant baptism serve?

Here Backus was thrown back upon the covenant theology which lay at the heart of New England Puritanism. According to the New England version of the covenant theology the agreement which God made with Abraham to save him and all of his descendants in Israel if they would live up to His laws was continued or transferred in the New Testament to all who believed that Jesus was the Son of God. God had expressly made his covenant with "Abraham and his seed"; and just as the feast of the Passover under the covenant with Abraham was the prototype for the Lord's Supper under the covenant with Christians, so infant baptism was "the gospel form of circumcision."

But the key point of the problem to the pietistic mind was the purpose for which circumcision or infant baptism had been practiced under the covenant. Backus was quite willing to accept the continuity of the covenant from the Old to the New Testament until Hinds and Woods pointed out the evil consequences of this theory of continuity in regard to the institutional structure of the church and its relationship to the state. In the first place, the Jewish church was clearly a national church, a theocracy in which Moses and Aaron ruled together, and thus the Puritans were able to utilize the covenant theology to justify their ecclesiastical laws and their system of territorial parishes and religious taxes. In the second place, the covenant theology provided the Puritans with justifications for the Halfway Covenant, thus polluting the purity of the mystical body of Christ. And in the third place the covenant theology, by emphasizing that grace ran "through the loins of godly parents," that the baptized children of visible saints were somehow more likely than others to obtain salvation, thereby established a kind of hereditary spiritual aristocracy; it also undermined the sovereignty of God by implying that God was bound by this covenant to save certain persons rather than others.

These arguments forced Backus to recognize that the Separates must explicitly reject the covenant theology. But to do this was to reject the whole conception of the corporate Christian state which the Puritans had so painstakingly constructed in the wilderness of New England. And it was just here that the Puritans had recognized the antipedobaptists as the "incendiaries of commonwealths."

The Puritans had said that the attempt to form pure churches of the converted was sheer fanaticism and arrogance. And the Separates, by continuing to baptize infants, would soon face the same problem the Puritans had when they adopted the Halfway Covenant in 1662: What status did a baptized infant have in a pure church after he came of age but was not converted? The Puritans had decided to abandon their earlier pietistic and perfectionist notion of a gathered church consisting only of visible saints. They had come to believe that religious education and nurture somehow prepared baptized infants for salvation. They had enacted ecclesiastical laws to preserve good order in the churches and to support them by compulsion, because they believed that God would be more willing to convert those who lived in a Christian Commonwealth. In short, the Puritans had conceived of Christianity in organic terms, as a process of growth and continuity—an evolutionary rather than a revolutionary process. And they disliked the Anabaptist view which left the continuity of the church and hence of the commonwealth up to the contingency of wholly adventitious conversions in adulthood. God's grace was miraculous but not fortuitous; no community, no corporate Christian state, could depend upon this kind of spasmodic action if it was to have stability and order. The Puritans feared the depravity of man too much to trust that God would be willing to save souls with sufficient regularity to preserve Christian civilization without considerable support and assistance from the institutions of Church and State. That was why He had ordained them.

It is doubtful whether Backus recognized all of the ramifications of this problem at the outset, but there is no doubt that it threw him into such spiritual anguish as he had never known before. Some years later he offered the following explanation for his delay in coming to a decision: "the hot disputes and vehement urgings that we had among us on both sides, occasion'd such tossings in my mind as seemed as if they would have sifted and shaken me, as it were, to pieces; after which I was much overwhelmed with melancholy and discouragements for a great while."

From August 7 to August 27, Backus "was crying to God for help and direction" regarding infant baptism until "it was So much press'd upon my mind that I preach'd upon it in the after-noon—that none had any right to baptism but Believers, and that plunging Sem'd the only right mode." This sermon produced consternation in his church, and Backus admitted in his diary that "before I had done I felt my mind entangled, and an awful gloom followed for twenty four hours." Then "my mind was turned back to infant baptism." His inability to come to a decision was typical of a host of Separates, lay and clerical, in these years. There seemed no way out of the dilemma. The arguments for the antipedobaptist position appeared extremely strong, yet to adopt them was to shatter the Separate movement just as it seemed about to succeed. Backus was wracked to the depths of his soul. He lost his close rapport with the Holy Spirit. The New Light no longer shone for him.

Almost as an escape from his perplexity, Backus turned to completing his plans for marriage to Susanna Mason of

Rehoboth. He had proposed to her on March 13, 1748/49 but no date had been set for the marriage. On September 22, after a trip to Norwich to consult with his family, he went to Rehoboth and agreed with Susanna upon a date late in November. He then returned to Titicut and made arrangements with the Fobes family to bring his bride there to live until such time as he could raise money to buy a home for her.

Susanna Mason was born in Rehoboth in 1724/25, the daughter of Samuel Mason, a yeoman. Samuel Mason's grandfather, Sampson Mason, had come to the Plymouth colony in the 1660's and had been a soldier in Oliver Cromwell's Roundhead Army. The family were Baptists, as were many in Rehoboth, and when Susanna was converted in 1745, she held antipedobaptist views though she joined the Separate Church which John Paine (brother of Solomon and Elisha of Canterbury) founded there in 1748. Perhaps her friendship with Backus, which began in 1746, had something to do with this. But she never hid her Baptist views, and Backus was fully aware of them when he asked her to marry him.

Little is known about Susanna, for she was, like so many ministers' wives in these years, completely self-effacing. Several of Backus's letters to her remain, but none of hers to him, and only two from her to her family. Backus preserved her account of her conversion on April 12, 1746, which he published in 1803. It is the common story of "a careless life . . . full of nothing but sin" until her confrontation with divine truth. The only biographical account of her was written by Backus as a tribute after her death. Here he describes her as a pietist would, primarily in terms of her spiritual character, her dedication to God, her faithfulness in rearing her children in a pious way, and her devotion to the duties of a wife and mother: "Her prudence and economy did much towards the support of our family . . . and her exemplary walk and conversation caused her to be highly esteemed by her acquaintance in general."

She must have been a very capable and thrifty woman, for she managed to raise nine children with comparatively little help from her husband (though at times he provided her with an apprenticed servant girl). Backus spent much of his time in travel, and even when he was at home he was often busy writing or with church duties. On her fell the tasks of maintaining the household, and without her strong, efficient help Backus would have had a far less productive and useful career. Nowhere in the diary or letters of Backus is there any hint of discord between them. If Susanna ever felt, as well she might have, a tinge of jealousy over her husband's close ties to his mother, she left no record of it. Her reward was a eulogy by her husband in a second edition of the funeral sermon he wrote for his mother and a memoir set side-by-side with that for Elizabeth Tracy Backus.

When Backus returned to Titicut on September 23 after having the banns for his marriage published in Rehoboth, he found to his surprise "that Ebenezer Moulton of Brimfield, a Baptis Preacher had ben here among my people a preaching and had Plung'd Some of them last Lordsday Sept. 17." Moulton had not wandered into Titicut by chance; he had been sent for by Hinds and Woods. Moulton (or Molten) was born in Windham, Connecticut in 1709 and according to Backus was descended from one of Ann Hutchinson's Antinomian followers. After his conversion he had joined a small Baptist church in Brimfield, Massachusetts, in 1736. In 1741 he was ordained and began a long and successful career as an itinerant which eventually took him to Nova Scotia. On this occasion he baptized nine of Backus's leading church members, including Hinds, Woods, William Hooper, and Nathaniel Shaw.

He also baptized Joseph Leach who was not a member
but who attended regularly. After leaving Titicut, Moulton went to Raynham and baptized three more persons.
"These things," said Backus when he learned of them,
"have made great Shakeings and Contentions among the
people and brought heavy Trials upon my Soul."

And well they might, for what was the church to do with
these persons who had broken their covenant to uphold
infant baptism? Backus had to make clear his own position.
He called a church meeting on September 26 "and I re-
tracted what I had preached against infant baptism, after
which disputes about it were often warm." Those who
had taken Backus's profession of antipedobaptism on August 27 seriously were especially offended with his retrac-
tion. "Brother Jonathan Woods and some others with
him (because of these things) separated from us and held
meetings by themselves." Now there were two New Light
churches in Titicut parish: one based on pedobaptist principles and one on antipedobaptist principles. Woods was
joined by Ebenezer Hinds, Joseph Harvey and his wife,
Timothy Briant, Joseph Leach, and Nathaniel Shaw. Ebenezer Moulton returned and helped them form a church
and then signed certificates stating that they were bona
fide Baptists and entitled to exemption from religious
taxes in Titicut. But the parish assessors refused to consider persons who separated from the Separates to be true
Baptists; they were merely a factional schism from Backus's
church. Most Separate-Baptist churches which were
formed in New England over the next few decades had
similar difficulties in convincing the Standing Order that
they were Baptists under the terms of the exemption act
of 1728 and its successors. This little Separate-Baptist
Church in Titicut lasted only until May, 1750. Then it
dissolved and its members joined either the Baptist church
in Swansea or the Second Baptist Church in Boston (their

certificates from these churches were honored by the Titicut assessors).

After the departure of the antipedobaptists Backus tried
to pull his remaining members together. At the Sunday
service on October 8, "I Spake a few words of my Sorrow
for my preaching against believers bringing their children
to baptism and Shewed how my Soul was now Satesfied
in that point." Then one of the members brought forward
her child for baptism and Backus performed the rite by
sprinkling, as he had always done.

On Wednesday, November 29, Backus was married. He
refused to permit any of the frivolous merrymaking or
frolicking which normally accompanied marriages in New
England, because he considered it a solemn ordinance of
God. "I have often Looked with abhorance upon the
Comon Practis of most people in this Point: namely their
giveing way to their Lusts and indulging themselves in
vanity and Carnality when they are about to Seek a Companion and to Enter into a married State." Susanna agreed
with him. The wedding took place in her father's house
in Rehoboth and was performed by a justice of the peace
in accordance with the prevailing custom. But Backus received permission of the justice to have his friends transform it into a religious ceremony:

Br. Shepheard read a Psalm and we Sung; then we went to
prayer and the Lord did hear and Come near to us. Then I
took my dear Sister Susanna by the Hand and Spoke Something
of the Sense I had of our Standing and acting in the presence
of God, and also how that he had Clearly Pointed out to me
this Person to be my Companion and an helper meet for me.
And Then went on and declar'd the marriage Covenant: and
She did the same to me. Then Esq. Foster Solemnly declar'd
that we were Lawfull man and Wife: then Brother Shepherd
went on to wish us a blessing and gave us a Sweet Exortation.
And So Did some others; then brother Paine Pray'd and had

freedom therein. Then I read, and we Sung the 101 Psalm after that I preach'd a Short Sermon from Acts 13:36.

The couple spent the next two days in Rehoboth and on Saturday "came home to Bridgwater."

But his marriage brought him no nearer to a solution in the debate over baptism. On February 16 he wrote in his diary, "there appear'd a Light in the North, more bright than has appear'd this Some years, like that Spoken of in Joel 3. Blood and Fire and Pillers of Smoke. . . . O! that remembering this wormwood and Gall my Soul might always be humbled in me! Alas I feel like Such a guilty Retch I know not what to do with my Self! God be merciful to me a Sinner!"

His church was in such a state of turmoil that for months on end the members neglected to hold communion together. Among these pietists communion was possible only when the church was at peace and the saints could commune with one another and with God in harmony. Those who were still pedobaptists thought that Backus and the church should take disciplinary action against the antipedobaptists for breach of their covenant. On September 2, "I told the Church that I was satesfied that we had ben wrong in neglecting the Lords-Supper and the Disapline of the Church because Some of us wan't Clearly Satesfied concerning Infant Baptism." The church voted to hold communion on the next Sabbath. It was the first time in twelve months; "But some withdrew and did not Pertake. . . . the Lord Pity this People. In the evening I felt guilty and Perplex'd. . . ."

In October he made a preaching tour of Cape Cod, hoping to spread the Separate doctrines and help form a church there. He also took a trip to Boston to sell some of his farm produce and some of his brother Elijah's ironware from the family ironworks at Yantic in Norwich. But business dealings took his mind off spiritual concerns. "Through most of this week," he wrote on October 26, 1750, "I've been Considerably Comber'd with Worldly concerns, which Sometimes does much to distress my soul."

Susanna was now pregnant and Backus decided to move his family into a house of its own. After looking around Backus decided to buy the house and farm of James Keith of Middleborough. It was in Titicut parish and was in fact the same house from which Keith had forbade him to preach when he had formed the Separate Church. It took him four months to raise enough money to complete the transaction. "It is a diffacult time about money and Some of my friends have thought me venturesome thus to run into Debt." Had he not been able to sell some of the land he had inherited in Norwich and Canterbury he could never have managed it.

Few of the Separate ministers had his inherited wealth to fall back upon; and it goes far to account for the stability of his church and the productivity of his career in later years that he was not obliged to depend upon his church for support nor to devote all of his energies to farming or trade in order to support his family. Backus never faced abject poverty. In addition to the income from rent of his land in Norwich and Canterbury, he had the income from his farm, from the trade he carried on as agent for Elijah's ironworks, and from book-selling, a business in which many ministers engaged at that period.

Less than a week after Backus signed the papers to buy the Keith farm, Susanna gave birth to their first child, on November 8, 1750. When her "distress Came on about 10 or 11 O'clock" Backus rushed out and "fetch'd Granney Clap," the local midwife. Her labor "continu'd and increas'd all the night after—till they were almost redy to Dispair of Deliverance. But we were brought to Cry to God in this hour of trouble and he did appear in his mercy. She was deliver'd of a daughter about half an hour Before Sun-rise this morning. And the Life of both Mother and Child is Spar'd and Seam as well as we Can expect. . . . my Soul also was much moved" with "a Concideration of the new Relation which I am now Brought into, as well as the thoughts of another Imortal Soul's being Brought into an evil World. . . ." They named the child Hannah. Four sons and four more daughters were born to them at regular intervals over the next eighteen years. Backus was luckier than most in seeing all of them grow to maturity.

Backus, his wife and child moved into the Keith house on March 19, 1751. A few weeks later, while itinerating on Cape Cod with Elder William Carpenter of the Separate Church in Bridgewater, Backus came face to face with the hazards of traveling preaching. The Rev. Ephraim Avery and the Rev. Abner Lewis, the Standing ministers in Truro and Billingsgate, confronted them, and Avery "ask'd what right We had to preach in his parish without his leave." Massachusetts had no law against itinerancy as Connecticut did, but there were other ways to imprison the unwanted. His friend, Elisha Paine, had been confined in Worcester jail in 1743 on charges of vagrancy while preaching in Woodstock. Other itinerants had been jailed for "disturbing the peace." Backus refused to be frightened off, however. Lewis engaged him in a debate which lasted for two and a half hours. A crowd gathered, most of whom seemed to sympathize with Backus. Lewis, seeing that he was not helping his cause, departed without calling the constable. Since Backus's preceding visit to the Cape, a Separate church had been formed in Harwich and the Standing ministers in the vicinity were fearful that the movement would spread into their parishes, as indeed it did.

The Separate movement was spreading in Middleborough, too. James Mead, a member of Backus's church, had been preaching in the southern part of the town known as Beech Woods, about twelve miles from Backus's church. He had made a number of converts who found it too long a journey to travel on foot for regular attendance at Backus's church. They therefore sought permission to form their own church and hold services nearer to their homes with Mead as their pastor. Backus's church considered this request on May 26, 1751, and granted it. In addition, there were no Separate churches in Norton, Rehoboth, Harwich, and Attleborough, and in other parts of Massachusetts and Connecticut.

Backus had now debated with himself and his church members for almost two years about baptism, and on July 20, 1751, he finally decided that he must resolve the issue in his own mind once and for all. "After confessing his sin and earnestly imploring divine help, he took Wilson's Scripture Manual and seriously examined every particular passage of God's Word which relates to baptism and was forced to 'give in' that the sentiments of Mr. Wilson [a Baptist] appeared to be according to the mind of Christ. Then, still looking to the Most high for direction, he went on to examine several portions of the Sacred Record, which speak of God's blessing his people and their seed with them. He carefully reviewed the account of Noah's preservation with his family, the promises made to Abraham and his seed, to David and his posterity, and the descriptions given in the Old Testament of the Messiah's reign; and he concluded . . . that God had promised to manifest himself to his people in the latter days, and to pour out his Spirit upon them in a very extraordinary and glorious manner; also that he had given to believers great encouragment to bring their offspring to him, praying and hoping for large blessings upon them; 'for they shall all know him, from the least to the greatest.'

But he was led at the same time by this comprehensive and prayerful survey to conclude that none ought to be baptized, and thus have the outward mark of Christ's disciples put upon them, except those who give evidence of having believed in him. This settlement of the question gave him some degree of peace. 'But yet alas!' he says, 'I feel like a weak creature still, having but little strength and boldness to come forth in the truth in this evil day.' "

Backus told the church on July 25 that he was no longer able to believe that God commanded infant baptism. There seemed only one way out of the resulting confusion. "Considering Our broken & dificult Circumstances we agreed to send for advice & Council to the [Separate] Churches in Norwich, Canterbury, Plainfield, Providence & Cambridge Norwest Parish to come & meet with us for that Purpose." Meanwhile Backus took a trip to the Northwest Parish of Cambridge to consult with Nathaniel Draper, a graduate of Yale and the pastor of an open-communion Separate-Baptist Church in which the question of antipedobaptism was considered a matter of individual choice.

This relieved Backus's mind and on August 22, almost without premeditation, he took the final step and allowed himself to be immersed: "Brother Benjamin Pierce, Pastor of a Church in part of Warwick [Rhode Island], preached among us at brother Hindses this Day with Considerable Power; and then in the Afternoon Concluded to Baptize Some Persons. Now in the morning I had Tho'ts of going to a meeting at Norton To day but Providence Sem'd to shut up The way; So I went to this meeting; and tho' I felt dreadful Struggles in my mind About many things in the morning—Yet I had Sweet Refreshings under his preaching: and when I came to see him Baptize Sundry persons, I haveing been convinced before that the Way that I us'd to go on in, In Baptizing Infants and by Sprinkling was not according to Scripture—and having this oppertunity to Practice as I now believ'd Was right—I darn't put it off: therefore I told Some account of my Conversion and Then of my experiences as to these Things, which gave Satesfaction; then I went down Into the Water with him and was Baptiz'd. And both then and Afterwards in the evening I felt a sweet Calmness of mind and some things open'd with Special clearness to my Soul."

Backus later published his reasons for adopting anti-pedobaptist principles in a tract entitled *A Short Description of the Difference Between the Bond-Woman and the Free; As They Are the Two Covenants. . . . Wherein Is Particularly Shewn That None Are Proper Subjects of the Special Ordinances of the Gospel-Church But Real Saints* (Boston, 1756). In this tract he rejected the covenant theology of the Puritans by arguing as the Baptists had long done that the Bible contained not one covenant but two. The first of these was the old covenant of works made with the Jews, and the second was the covenant of grace made with those who believe in Christ. The people and the events of the Old Testament foreshadowed the work of Christ and the apostles in the New Testament—the gospel or Christian church is the anti-type of the Jewish church or Israel and Jesus Christ is the anti-type of Abraham. Backus and the Baptists stressed the discontinuity, the antithetical nature of the two, the complete and distinct break between the past and the present dispensations. That Americans were ready to grasp this new outlook after 1740 and to pursue it to its logical conclusions marks the real break with the Old World, the medieval mind, and the Puritan ethos. The Baptist doctrine of the two covenants was the pietistic formulation of the Enlightenment's rejection of the past, its willingness to cut all traditional ties with the old order and begin anew.

Backus's detailed refutation of the pedobaptist arguments contained nothing that was new to the Baptists and he borrowed most of his arguments from the noted English Baptist scholar John Gill. What was new was its espousal by a man who had grown up in the Puritan tradition; many others who had grown up in that tradition came to the same conclusions at the same time. Backus's re-statement of the Baptist position, expressed in the mood of the Separates' pietistic revolt against the Standing Order, completely rejuvenated the "Old Baptists" of New England, who, in the century between 1640 and 1740, had become so acculturated to the Puritan ethos as to deny at first any relationship with the New or Separate-Baptists.

The Bond-woman and the Free pointed out that the old covenant of the Jewish law was a covenant of works and ceremonies which typified the inability of man, since the fall, to obey the will of God. "One great thing designed in those ceremonies was to show the heinous nature and great evil of sin and thereby to discover more clearly man's awful and helpless Condition and his necessity of Christ." Because the Jews could not live up to the law and refused to accept Christ, they ceased to be God's chosen people. A new covenant, the covenant of grace, came into being with the birth of Christ and "the new patent . . . given to Jesus Christ, the antitype of Abraham, . . . is justly called 'a better covenant, established upon better promises,' Heb. viii.6." This new plan of salvation by faith freed men from the requirements of the Jewish law and gave them "freedom of approach to God thro' Jesus Christ."

Backus indicted the Puritan theory of the convenant "for jumbling the constitution of the old testament church and the new together; whereas if we take them distinct, the limits of each are exprest very plain." The Puritans' confusion had led them to try to establish an Old Testament Israel in New England; it led them to the baptism of children through the false analogy with circumcision; and it led them to the view that the Lord's Supper was "a con-verting ordinance" to which all upright persons should be admitted. Thus the Puritans had confused the gospel of grace with the doctrine of works and transformed the gospel church of visible saints into a national church with a birthright membership.

The Puritans, with their penchant for continuity and organic growth, found the perfect text to support the over-arching unity of the Abrahamic covenant in Romans 11:17. Here the apostle Paul spoke of the Christian cove-nant as being grafted on to the Jewish covenant as a branch is grafted on to an olive tree, from whence the Puritans "argued the right of professors now to baptize their chil-dren, because the Jews circumcized theirs." This Backus rejected as a misinterpretation. "The Jews were broken off thro' unbelief, and the Gentiles were graffed in, and stand only by faith." Faith was essential to baptism. What the Puritans stressed as organic continuity, Backus and the Baptists stressed as a complete break.

One other metaphor emphasized the complete rejection of tradition in Backus's Separate-Baptist theology and the willingness of the evangelicals to trust in the immediacy of the Spirit of God. Discussing Paul's reference to the Old Testament dispensation as "the Letter" of the law and the New Testament as the Spirit, Backus noted that the Jewish church "had a literal house and temple where God's name was fixed and his worship confined. . . . That old temple was built with stones. . . . that was a worldly sanctuary. . . ." It was worldly both by being in this world and by being solid, fixed, confined in a rigid and specific structure. "But in the new-testament we are confined to no place but the saints are God's house." Here the anti-institutional quality of the pietistic revolt against Puritanism meshed clearly with the new openness both of American society and with the mind of the Enlightenment. These underlying assumptions of the Revolutionary spirit, said Backus at the conclusion of his book, "I have found by experience."

The council of ministers and lay messengers which met at Titicut on October 2, 1751 to settle the problems of Backus's church was purely advisory. Yet by long tradition its moral force was such that its recommendations were certain to be accepted. *Ad hoc* councils of ministers and laymen had been used in New England from its beginning as the most effective means of maintaining order and harmony among the Puritan churches without destroying their congregational autonomy. The only sanction under this system was the denial of fellowship with other churches in the denomination. But this was generally sufficient, given the desire of those who sought the council to find a way out of their difficulty.

Those who made up the council of October 2 were Elders Solomon Paine of Canterbury, Thomas Stevens of Plainfield, Jedidiah Hide of Norwich, and Nathaniel Draper of Cambridge; and five laymen who were elected by these same churches to accompany their pastors. The latter were called "messengers" and were given equal votes with the elders on the council. Solomon Paine was the acknowledged leader of the Separate movement at this time and remained so until his death in 1754. A man of commanding presence and strong will, he had been a prominent citizen in Canterbury and a member of the legislature prior to joining the Separates in 1745. Several times he presented petitions to the Connecticut legislature demanding religious liberty for the Separates, and when these were ignored he was chosen by the Separates in 1754 to go to England to petition the King. He also published in 1752 one of the most forceful and extensive defenses of the Separate movement. Since his judgment was esteemed by all of the Separates, he was chosen moderator of the council in Titicut and wrote up its recommendation or "result."

After two days of deliberation the council concluded that both Backus and his church had "failed to put the Laws of Christs House in Execution" by censuring covenant-breakers, and that Backus himself was a "transgressor" because he had "violated his Pastoral Covenant" requiring him to keep the church in good order. But nowhere in the result did the council deal with the question of antipedobaptism. The issue was still too sensitive to be handled decisively. The advice to the Titicut church was that the members should "renew covenant" with one another and, in effect, start afresh, letting by-gones be bygones. "Those that Refused to covenant to walk with those who did renew Covenant," however, were to be censured and "deem'd persons of an Irregular Standing."

In effect this recommendation implied that antipedobaptism was not in itself a cause for censure. In urging Backus's members to renew covenant and go on together as a church, the council implicitly endorsed a policy of open communion; i.e., Backus, like Nathaniel Draper, was to minister to pedobaptists and antipedobaptists alike and the proper subjects and mode of baptism were to be considered "extra-fundamental" or "non-essential" details. This decision was not surprising. The Separate Church in Mansfield, Connecticut, one of the first of the new denomination to adopt and publish a set of articles of faith, had stated in 1745, "Though most of us agree in the Article of Infant baptism, yet a difference in that particular doth not break the spiritual communion of saints; therefore it is no just bar to our covenanting and partaking of the ordinances together wherein we are agreed." This, along with the other articles in the Mansfield statement, had been adopted by many other Separate churches formed since that time. Even Solomon Paine had admitted to his church some members who opposed infant baptism.

But while the members of Backus's church took the advice of the council and sixteen of them renewed covenant together on an open communion basis, this compromise position proved to be no longer viable. Part of the difficulty was that Backus, though the pastor to both groups, was himself strictly committed to the antipedobaptist position. He therefore refused to baptize the infants of his pedobaptist brethren (though he said he had no objection to their being baptized by any other Separate minister). This antagonized two of the more fervent pedobaptists, Samuel Alden and Robert Washburn, and they refused to accept him as a proper pastor of the church. For this they were censured by the majority and denied the right to take communion with the church. Considering that they had been wrongly treated, Alden and Washburn demanded that another council hear their side of the case. Meanwhile, Ebenezer Hinds and the other antipedobaptists who had withdrawn from the church and were now attending Baptist churches in Boston or Swansea, refused to renew covenant on an open-communion basis. The church therefore placed them under censure too. Thus the church, far from being reunited by the compromise, was now divided from both sides, and only a small minority was willing to accept the open communion policy which Backus and the council had favored.

A second council at Titicut on May 25, 1752, proved unable to resolve the difficulty. While it agreed with Alden and Washburn that the church was wrong in censuring them, it also agreed with Backus that Alden and Washburn were wrong to refuse to accept him as their pastor. The result of this council stated only that "the pastor and church as a body lay under the defilement of sin in neglecting to go on in gospel discipline." But it did not

offer any way out of the dilemma. The church struggled
on for a time and then in September, 1752, decided to excommunicate Alden and Washburn for refusing to relent
in their attitude toward Backus.

In view of the fact that the preceding council had stated
that the church ought not to have censured them in the
first place, Alden and Washburn now felt so badly treated
that they called a council to exonerate themselves. This
council met at Titicut on November 1, 1752. Solomon
Paine was again moderator; Thomas Stevens, Joseph
Snow, and Elder Alexander Miller of the Separate
Church in Voluntown, together with four lay messengers,
constituted the council. Strictly speaking, Backus and the
church need not have accepted the jurisdiction of an
ex parte council called by the two aggrieved brethren, but
they did so in the belief that they could sustain their position and perhaps bring the two back into the fold. But to
his great consternation, the result of the council exoner-
ated Alden and Washburn and condemned Backus and
the church. In fact, the council explicitly condemned the
practice of open communion, thereby reversing the whole
trend of the Separate movement and instituting a breach
which proved its downfall.

Backus wrote that the result was "exceeding conterary
to my expectation" and wholly inconsistent with the first
council of October 2, 1751. He could not understand why
Paine and Stevens, who had served on both councils,
had reversed their positions. "I went on to Reason with
'em for Some time," Backus wrote in his diary, "for we had
held heretofore that a difference in judgment about Baptism was no Bar of Communion. . . . And they held that
it was so, if persons plainly denied it [i.e., the validity of
infant baptism]; but yet as to private members that appeared to be sincerely following God but hadn't Light on
Infant Baptism, they held that such might be receiv'd in

the church." On the other hand, Paine and Stevens were agreed that they would no longer hold fellowship with confirmed antipedobaptists; nor did they think it possible for an antipedobaptist, like Backus, to remain pastor of a Separate Church.

A majority of Backus's church members proceeded to reinstate Alden and Washburn and censure Backus. Now it was the turn of Backus and his minority to call an *ex parte* council which met in Titicut on January 31, 1753. It found "a peculiar difficulty subsisting among them which affects the whole number of the Separate churches," and therefore refused to give a judgment "until the number of the faithful, by their messengers meet together in a general assembly to settle points of communion." In short, there was no point in multiplying councils. The issue was one affecting the whole denomination, and it should be decided by the representatives of all the Separates meeting together in what the seventeenth century Puritans would have called a Synod.

Thus Backus emerged as the leader of the Separate-Baptist faction within the radical New Light movement. For the next three years he and his faction vied with the closed-communion pedobaptists, under Solomon and Elisha Paine and Thomas Stevens, for the allegiance of the pietists of the new reformation. Backus wished to hold the denomination together by preserving the policy of open communion while holding the door open for "further light." Perhaps the whole movement would swing to his position if the denomination's creed, practice, and structure could remain flexible for just a little longer.

The synod met in Exeter, Rhode Island, on May 23, 1753. It included delegates from twenty-five churches from Massachusetts and Connecticut. Upon its decision hung the fate of another one hundred or more Separate congregations in New England. After two days of discussion and

debate the delegates agreed with only one dissenting voice
to adhere to the policy of open communion. This decision
was a great victory for Backus. But its force was considerably weakened by the absence from the conference of the
leading members of the closed-communion party, notably
Solomon and Elisha Paine and Thomas Stevens, who then
had no choice but to call another representative conference or synod to meet in Stonington, Connecticut, on May
29, 1754.

Meanwhile Backus's church in Titicut was reorganized
once again upon an open communion basis. On July 12,
1753, the church voted to retract its excommunication
of Alden and Washburn and its censure of Hinds and the
antipedobaptists on the grounds that "in such cases that
persons plead they are consciencious in, and their other
conduct appears agreeable, We ought not to censure them,
but rather exercise forebareance towards them & labour
in Love for their enlightening. . . ." Neither group, however, received sufficient enlightenment to return to the
fold prior to the Stonington Conference.

This conference was the largest convention of the Separates ever to be held. The new denomination was at its
height in numbers and enthusiasm. Though wracked with
internal disputes about baptism and persecuted bitterly
from without by distraint of goods and imprisonments
for refusing to pay religious taxes, the movement was full
of faith, hope, and fervor. Numbering over 125 organized congregations and uncounted enclaves of smaller
groups, the denomination was a phenomenon of astound-
ing proportions in the tightly-ordered corporate life of
New England. Continued growth at the same rate for another decade would have ensured the complete overthrow
of the parish system. In some parishes, like Benjamin
Lord's in Norwich, the Separates were already a majority; and since they retained the legal right to vote in par-

ish meetings, they were completely disrupting the system by refusing to vote the annual taxes for the support of the Standing minister.

Forty Separate churches sent a total of seventy-seven delegates to Stonington. Solomon Paine stated the case for closed communion pedobaptist principles. He "confest that when he join'd with the Baptist Bretherin in Communion . . . he didn't so critically examine into the foundation of things as he ought and he tho't then that they might go together in communion as he now found they cou'd not." He then put the case bluntly when he said (reading from a paper written by his brother Elisha), that either the pedobaptist "sins in making infants the subjects of baptism" or the antipedobaptist sins "in cutting them off" from baptism. There could be no two ways about it. No compromise with sin was possible. Baptism was too important an ordinance of the church to be a matter of indifference.

I pray God to pinch up our minds, until the troubler be found [who brought this controversy into our churches]; for it is not a division between Paedo and Antipaedobaptists, but promiscuously runs through the body of Christians, and will rend all cords of union between the dear lambs of God but what are made by human and party bands. Oh! my dear brethren! If God hath cut off infants by forbidding water to be put on them, let us never tolerate the practice of putting it on; but if not, let none dare to forbid it, but do it in proper office and time.

This speech won the battle but lost the war. The delegates in effect voted, thirty-seven to thirty-five (with six abstentions), to adopt a denominational policy of closed communion (or non-communion with antipedobaptists). The majority conceded only that they were willing to hold communion with Christians "who wanted light for infant baptism," i.e., who were still uncertain about its correctness. But they could not compromise with those who insisted that the new light of the new reformation had put an end to infant baptism as a corruption of primitive Christian practice.

Backus was shattered by the decision. He must now part with all of those saints in Norwich and many elsewhere who had come out from the Standing Order with him and whom he had loved, honored, and admired ever since. In later years he was to engage in some bitter pamphlet disputes with Separates elders like Ebenezer Frothingham and Israel Holly over these matters. But he had the grim satisfaction of watching the once powerful Separate movement wither away after 1754 while the Baptist movement grew steadily stronger.

The leadership of the open-communion faction of the Separate movement now fell upon Backus. And if the voting at the Stonington Conference was a fair indication, this was close to half of the denomination. A conference of his supporters at Exeter, Rhode Island, on September 10, 1754, declared in favor of open-communion. This decision came in the form of an affirmative vote in answer to the question, "Whether, if a Congregational [i.e., Separate] brother should come to a Baptist church in the fellowship of the gospel, and desire to commune with them at the Lord's table, but two or three refused to sit down with him—whether said church will receive that brother to communion or not?" The reason offered was "because we dare not shut out such as Christ evidently receives." Or, to put it another way, the fact that a man was a born-again Christian was more important than the views he held about baptism.

During the next year Backus strove to keep the Separate movement united, or at least to keep open the possibility of reunion between his faction and that of the Paines. But matters simply went from bad to worse. Separate churches everywhere became involved in the same quarrels which had wracked his own church in Titicut. And the various councils called to settle these quarrels gave conflicting decisions, according to whether they were dominated by delegates with open- or closed-communion views. At the same time, persecution of the Separates by the Standing Order increased in intensity. Tax assessors, finding the movement so riddled with internal confusion, decided to ignore its claims to exemption even when made by Separates who had adopted antipedobaptist principles.

With the conflict at its height, the Separates made their most determined bid to obtain exemption under the leadership of Solomon Paine in Connecticut and Richard Seaver in Massachusetts. Paine's effort began with a petition to the General Assembly signed by the representatives of twenty-two Separate churches in the colony. The petitioners stated that "we Believe it unequal that we should be Obliged to maintain a worship different from Ours" because "it is against our Consciences that Ministers Sallaries should be dependent on human Laws Enforced by Taxes, Impositions &c. Because we find neither Example nor Precept for it in the word of God [and] we Believe it has a natural tendency to make ministers mercenary, to introduce Hierlings into the Sacred Office and to make marchandize of the Gospell of Christ." The General Assembly dismissed the petition in May, 1754 (as the General Assembly of Massachusetts did the one submitted by the Separates there at the same time). Paine and the Separates then drafted a long memorial "To the Kings Most Excellent Majesty in Council." One thousand signers, who described themselves as "Loyal and Dutifull Subjects to your Majesty who Detest & abhor all ye Romish Superstition and are for ye most part Heads of Famalies and Freemen," protested that it was contrary to "ye Toleration Acts" that they should "suffer Persecution from Their Brethren ["Presbyterian or Consociated"] who Also Profess Themselves Dissenters from ye Church of England." And they prayed that they might not be "Hereafter Compelled to make or yeald to any such Taxes for ye Maintainance of sd Established Ministers of Meeting Houses" in Connecticut.

Paine, however, died shortly thereafter, so that not until April 15, 1756, did two representatives of the Connecticut Separates, Bliss Willoughby and Moses Morse, embark for England. Before presenting the memorial to the King the emissaries sought the advice of a political lobby elected by the Baptist, Independent, and Presbyterian churches in London to protect the interests of the dissenters by pressure on Parliament. The Dissenting Deputies, as this group was called, advised Willoughby and Morse not to present the memorial to the King, who might only use it as an excuse for taking away the charter of Connecticut. Dr. Benjamin Avery, the chairman of the Dissenting Deputies, suggested instead that they return to Connecticut and bring a suit through the courts for their rights. He also promised to write a letter to the governor and his council reprobating in strong terms their intolerance and persecution. Willoughby and Morse took his advice; but Avery's letter to Governor Fitch did no good, and the lawsuit eventually lapsed. Not until 1777 did Connecticut finally grant exemption to the Separates on the same terms as those for Baptists, Quakers, and Anglicans. And not until 1780 did they obtain relief in Massachusetts. By that time the denomination had diminished to a tiny handful of churches and no longer posed any threat to the Standing Order.

The reasons for the decline of the Separate movement are not difficult to explain. The more radical New Light pietists rapidly drifted into the Separate-Baptist ranks; and the more conservative returned to the fold as the established churches gradually abandoned the Halfway Covenant. Only those Separates who insisted on voluntarism or the abolition of compulsory religious taxes remained independent, and most of those pietists who felt strongly about this matter found the Baptist formulation of it more convincing.

Backus struggled for another year to maintain his church and the others in his faction upon an open-communion basis. He made his members agree not to bring up the touchy problem. He agreed to conduct dedication services for infants or to let pedobaptists bring in another minister for baptism by sprinkling. But this self-imposed restraint proved too hard for pietists to bear. They began to feel, as Solomon Paine had felt, that they were compromising with sin rather than rejoicing in charity. For that whole year, 1754-1755, they were so plagued with doubts that once again they could not attain the proper spiritual frame to hold communion together. By January, 1756, Backus was ready to give up the experiment with open-communion.

On January 2, he held a church meeting at his home and Ebenezer Hinds was present. "I now declared that I firmly believed that as none are the proper subject of baptism but real saints, so every such soul ought to be baptized by immersion before they come to the Lords Supper." He entreated his church members to form a new church on these principles. On January 16, the people met again and Brother Hinds preached to them on "how we ought to purge out the old leaven in order to be a new lump." Backus presented a new set of articles and a new covenant based upon closed-communion, antipedobaptist principles. After reading and discussing them, they were signed by Backus, "Timothy Briant and John Hayward, Mary Caswell, Esther Fobes and my dear consort."

And so the Separate Church in Titicut came to an end

so far as Backus was concerned. Those who still favored its pedobaptist principles continued to meet for a time, but they now spoke of themselves as the parish church and were ready to work with the precinct committee to find a minister agreeable both to Backus's former pedobaptist members and to the conservatives who had always opposed him. The man who consummated this happy reunion was the Rev. Solomon Reed, a Harvard graduate and former pastor of the Standing Church in Framingham, but an ardent New Light nonetheless. Some of Backus's former supporters hoped he would agree to settle on a basis of voluntary support. But he would not, and the parish agreed to lay taxes for his salary.

Backus and his church members were safe, however. They were now bona fide Baptists and entitled to the benefit of the tax exemption law.

IV

The Separate-Baptists
and the Old Baptists

---

*"I cou'dnt but admire to see ye doctrines of grace
bear such sway among these old Baptist Societyes
where Arminianism has almost universally prevail'd
for many years."* ISAAC BACKUS, "Diary," (1758)

WHEN BACKUS formed the First Baptist
Church in Middleborough on January 16, 1756, it was the
first of its type in the region. There were eighteen closed-
communion Baptist churches in the Puritan colonies at this
time, five of them in Connecticut and thirteen in Massachusetts. But most of these were "Old Baptists" who had
taken little part in the Awakening and were not in fellowship with the Separate-Baptist churches.

The first post-Awakening Baptist Church in Massachusetts was formed in 1742 when a group of Calvinistic New
Lights split off from the First Baptist Church of Boston
(founded in 1665). These New Lights charged that their
Harvard-educated pastor, Jeremiah Condy, was "an Arminian" who denied "the doctrines of election and predestination," who asserted "man's free will agency" in
conversion, and who was an enemy of the Awakening.

They were particularly "affrighted at a declaration in one of his sermons that Christians cannot know or distinguish the operation of the Spirit of God upon their souls from the operation of their own minds." Similar Arminian sentiments prevailed among most of the Old Baptist churches in New England.

Most of the other pre-Awakening Baptist churches in the colony were as cool toward the Awakening as the First Baptist Church of Boston. No new Baptist churches had been formed in Massachusetts between 1693 and 1731, the period of the ebb tide of colonial pietism. Then between 1731 and 1740 five Baptist churches were formed in the province, at Rehoboth (1731), Sutton (1733), South Brimfield (1736), Bellingham (1737), and Leicester (1738). Between 1740 and the founding of Backus's church four more, including the Second in Boston, were formed; the others were West Springfield (1740), Sturbridge (1741), and Rehoboth Second (1753). By and large these new tide churches were somewhat more Calvinistic in temper; but still they lacked the fervor, the leadership, and the dynamic spirit which animated the New Light Separate churches.

In addition to the theological cleavage between the Arminian and the moderately Calvinistic factions, the Baptists were also very much divided in practice in 1756, especially if one takes into account those in Rhode Island, which was the center of the denomination at this time. A small group of Seventh Day Baptist Churches had started in Newport in 1671 and spread to the western shore of Narragansett Bay around Hopkinton and Westerly. Eighteen or twenty Six Principle Baptist churches in that colony and in Connecticut and Massachusetts believed that no person could be admitted to membership until he had submitted to the ritual of laying on of hands, an ordinance which they found sanctioned in Hebrews 6:2. The

Five Principle Baptists either omitted the laying on of hands or considered it optional and non-essential. Arminianism, in the form of General Redemption, prevailed among the Six Principle Baptists but not among the Five Principle—though the distinction was by no means clearcut. The Seventh Day Baptists were generally Calvinistic.

Against all of these Baptists the Separates held the ingrained prejudices of their Puritan upbringing. The Baptists reciprocated this distrust, so that there was little or no intercourse between the two groups. Prior to 1756 Backus had virtually no contact even with the most Calvinistic of them.

After 1756 the situation changed rapidly. The Separate-Baptists and the Old Baptists were forced together by the terms of the tax exemption laws which, unrealistically but logically, lumped all antipedobaptists together as a single denomination. Furthermore, the two groups came together through their common beliefs, needs, and goals, especially their opposition to the established system. But in large measure the credit for overcoming the apathy, mistrust, and even hostility among the Baptists of all kinds was due to the unremitting efforts of Backus and a few other Separate-Baptist leaders.

The church which Backus started with six members in January, 1756, increased to eleven by March and fourteen in December. Six years later the membership had risen to fifty-two and by 1776 it numbered sixty-six. Because it depended upon a conversion experience which came only through the initiative of God and could not be induced in any way by man, the actual membership of such churches was never large. The congregations of "regular attenders" who formed the "society" were usually three to five times as numerous; but the regular attenders had not experienced grace and could not be immersed or admitted to communion. It was always a sticky legal point therefore, whether they as well as the immersed members of the Baptist churches were exempt from religious taxes.

By 1762 Backus's Baptist Church had as many full members, however, as Solomon Reed's parish church in Titicut. In addition, Backus helped to establish two other Baptist churches in Middleborough, both of them offshoots of his own. In 1757 Ebenezer Hinds founded one in the Lakeville region, nine miles south of Backus's church. The other, formed in 1761 with Ebenezer Jones as pastor, was located eleven miles southeast of Backus's church and by 1762 had forty-eight members.

Thus within six years after Backus's emergence as a closed-communion Baptist, Middleborough had the largest concentration of Separate-Baptists of any town in New England. All three churches built meetinghouses and bought parsonages and farms for their pastors. But because Hinds and Jones lacked Backus's independent wealth and also his abilities as a farmer and trader, they were not able to live comfortably on the meager freewill offerings of their congregations. It became one of the chronic and difficult problems of the Baptists to provide adequate support for their pastors in the eighteenth century, even though most of them, like Backus, worked in a worldly vocation for their incomes. The paucity and poverty of their members, a stinginess motivated by New England tradition, and an avowed opposition to "a hireling ministry," induced Baptists to give money to their ministers only as an act of charity and not out of any sense of obligation. They had cried out so hotly against compulsory religious tax support and insisted so vehemently that ministers follow the Biblical text, "freely ye have received, freely give," that they would not regard ministerial support as a Christian obligation. The inability of the Baptists to support their ministers adequately was later used as proof that voluntarism would never sustain religious worship.

However, the Baptist movement thrived on the fact that its adherents were free from the burden of ecclesiastical taxes, and that its ministers were self-supporting and spoke the language of the common people. Egalitarian, anti-institutional, and anticlerical, it shared the belief in the priesthood of all believers, in lay ordination, and in lay participation through the exercise or improvement of spiritual gifts in preaching and prayer. Backus drew on these shared pietistic beliefs in his efforts for Baptist unity.

Backus early faced the problem of finding some Baptist churches and elders to assist at his ordination. He decided to pay a visit to the Baptist churches nearest to him, those in Rehoboth and Swansea. Ebenezer Hinds went with him, and they stopped first at the house of Elder Richard Rounds, the pastor of the Second Baptist Church in Rehoboth. "We found elder Rounds to be quite clear as to the doctrines of grace tho' he appear'd very strait-laced as to joining in any social worship with Christians of different sentiments from himself." Whether this meant that Rounds did not wish to have fellowship with Separate-Baptists or only that he refused to exchange pulpits with Six Principle and Arminian Baptists was not clear.

On February 10, Backus and Hinds went to Swansea and had "some discourse" with Elder Wood, Deacon Peck, and others of the First Baptist Church there. He found "there are a number who are as clear both as to doctrine and experience here as any Christians I meet with but then they own that there are some in their Church who are dark as to both, tho' they don't know what to do with 'em." Here was a church that might be persuaded to reform itself by censuring those who were lax in their Calvinism or persuading them of the correctness of "the doc-

trines of grace"; then it could enter into fellowship with
the Separate-Baptists. He and Hinds then went to the First
Baptist Church in Rehoboth, which seemed rather hope-
lessly Arminian, denying the doctrines of election and predestination and preaching that Christ died for all men. As
a result of this lax attitude toward "free grace" many of
the Arminian churches, Backus discovered, admitted almost anyone into membership who believed in antipedobaptism, whether or not he claimed to have had a conversion experience.

After returning home, Backus wrote, "I have now had
some acquaintance with three old Baptist Churches that I
was a stranger to before, and [while] I find some dear
Saints in each of 'em, others appear very dark. But I think
elder Round's Church is the clearest; oh, that God wo'd
cleanse 'em all more thoroughly!" He declared that he
would ask Elder Round to assist at his ordination, and he
wrote to Elder Ephraim Bound's Second Baptist Church
in Boston which he knew by reputation to be Calvinistic.
The two other Baptist elders whom he and his church
agreed to ask to serve on the ordination council were Peter
Werden of Warwick and David Sprague of Exeter, both
New Lights who had come out from Arminian Baptist
churches and formed Calvinistic churches of their own.
The ordination took place on June 23, 1756, "before a
great Congregation of people" in Titicut and "thro' the
whole exercise," said Backus, "my soul felt a great solem-
nity." Elder Noah Alden of the Separate-Baptist Church
in Stafford, Connecticut, also attended the service, though
he had arrived in Titicut only by accident at that moment.
Backus and Alden became good friends, and later, when
Alden became pastor in Bellingham, Massachusetts, worked
closely together to separate Church and State.

Between 1756 and 1760 Backus was concerned principally with his own church affairs. At first the church met

in his home; but this soon became too crowded. Then an addition was built to his barn so that services could be held there. Finally, in December, 1756, his congregation decided to build a meetinghouse. Since the attenders came from many different parts of the surrounding towns, there was contention about the most convenient site. But it was settled amicably when Paul Hathaway, one of the members, donated a section of his land in north Middleborough not far from Backus's home. Then came the arduous tasks of raising the funds and clearing the land, obtaining the timber and supplies, and performing the labor. Backus participated in every phase of the work. The frame of the building did not go up until December, 1757, and, as was typical of all New England house-raisings, two gallons of rum were provided by the church to inspirit the workers. The first meeting was not held in the meetinghouse until June 2, 1758, when the building still lacked a permanent roof. Backus noted in his diary six weeks later that the congregation "agreed to go next Friday with as many hands as they cou'd get to the Swamp to mak[e] Stuff [rushes] to cover our meeting house." The last item to be completed was the installation of the glass for the window panes, an expensive project. Then the pews were auctioned off and the church settled down happily in the quarters it occupied for the rest of Backus's life.

Meanwhile Backus continued to make trips to the churches in the surrounding towns, trying to build up the denomination and to persuade the Old Baptists to adopt Calvinistic views. He noted in his diary on February 2, 1758, after preaching in Rehoboth and Swansea, "I cou'dnt but admire to see ye doctrines of grace bear such sway among these old Baptist Societyes where Arminianism has almost universally prevail'd for many years." Backus also traveled to the new Separate-Baptist churches being formed by persons like himself who had previously been open-communion or pedobaptist Separates. He urged the open-communion churches to follow his example and adopt closed-communion policies, traveling so far as Newton, New Hampshire in March, 1756, to consult with a newly formed church there under the eldership of Thomas Walter Powers.

Wherever Backus heard of small groups which had adopted Baptist principles he went to see them, preach to them, nurture them until they had enough members to form a church—in Mendon, in Medfield, in Norton, in Attleborough, in Taunton, in Sutton, in Easton, in Rochester, and in most of the towns on Cape Cod. He by no means ignored the Baptists in Rhode Island and Connecticut, and on frequent trips to Norwich to visit his mother and brothers, he often made excursions to new groups in the vicinity. He was particularly successful in persuading those in the vicinity of Thompson, Stafford, Leicester, Spencer, Sturbridge, South Hadley and Framingham (who had formed an association under the leadership of Elder Wightman Jacobs) to give up the Sixth Principle.

From the list Backus kept of every journey taken and the number of miles traveled, it appears that between 1747 and 1806 he made 918 journeys ranging from twenty miles to 2,591 miles in length. He traveled in horseback with a small jug of rum in his saddlebag, and covered a total of 67,600 miles or an average of 1,200 a year. In many years he traveled over 2,000 miles. He delivered in this period 9,828 sermons, of which he also kept a careful record, preaching an average of four a week or 196 a year.

Backus did not undertake these trips aimlessly or just because the Spirit moved him. In most cases he had a definite destination in mind and a specific purpose: often he went in answer to requests for assistance, to participate in an ordination or to baptize some recent converts; sometimes he helped constitute a new church or settled disputes by participating in an *ad hoc* council. He early acquired a reputation for sound judgment and fair dealing as well as for the depth of his spiritual commitment, and he was much in request for peace-making missions in which he persuaded the disputants to pray with him for God's guidance. The Baptists had many troubles in the early days which called for a man with a firm grasp of fundamental principles and practices, one able to "divide the Scriptures" accurately and to place denominational interests above local factionalism. Given the strict congregational autonomy of the Baptists, stability and order rested upon the moral force of these *ad hoc* councils.

Backus was not always successful in restraining the more radical and perfectionist pietists. Ebenezer Ward, whom Backus described in 1757 as "a man of very bad character," felt moved by the Holy Spirit to preach and baptize in Attleborough, Norton, and Easton though he was never ordained. He persuaded a group to join him in forming a church whose members became so confident of their freedom from Satan's bondage that they decided they had become perfectly sinless. They also took literally the Biblical text that the saved would never die and declared themselves immortal. One of them told Backus that she had "pass'd thro' a change in her body equivalent to Death; so that She had ben intirely free[d] from any disorder in her Body or Corruption in her Soul ever since; and expected she ever sho'd be so; and that her Body wo'd never see Corruption but wo'd live here till Christ's personal coming." Several others declared that they were no longer bound by earthly, man-made laws meant only to control the unregenerate and impure, particularly by those concerning marriage. They felt free to abandon their lawful spouses and cohabit with spiritual soul mates. One gullible parent in Attleborough who permitted his daughter to do so, "for they lay with the Bible between them," learned to his chagrin that she became pregnant none-theless. Her husband, upon returning from a voyage, brought suit for divorce on grounds of adultery—not having received the new light on spiritual wifery. Backus did his best to fight this "antinomian" heresy and insisted that all those who had been baptized by unauthorized persons be re-baptized before they joined a regular Baptist church.

Other moral problems also threatened the movement in these early years. More than one elder became involved in cases of adultery and fornication, and several preachers seem to have been badly addicted to drink. Backus fought hard to preserve the reputation of the denomination by urging the censure or dismissal of such men and refused to accept the argument that it was a greater dishonor to the movement to expose such preachers publicly than to tolerate them silently.

However, most of the disputes he adjudicated were upon matters of church doctrine and discipline. He patiently explained to dozens of Baptist churches and individuals that the sixth principle, the seventh-day worship, footwashing, the Christian kiss, and other rites mentioned in the Bible were no longer applicable in contemporary churches. He argued that the proper gospel procedure must be followed whenever a church member was disciplined for some immoral or dishonest action. He had to see to it that petty disputes over tattling, back-biting, alleged slander, and "hard words" were not blown out of proportion. The pietists of the Separate-Baptist movement took very seriously their duty to be their brothers' keepers, and called to account before the church any who seemed to be departing from proper Christian behavior. Backus fully accepted the heavy responsibilities this obligation imposed. In some cases, however, the pietists carried their concern for their neighbor's behavior too far.

In Backus's own church, for example, one such dispute dragged on for many months. A woman had loaned two needles and some thread to a neighbor who did not return them, indeed denied that she had ever received them. In small New England communities such items of dispute soon became common gossip; families closed ranks behind the quarreling parties once the "slander" started to fly, and the ramifications for church and town affairs rapidly widened. Backus and other pietist pastors often wearied of these petty disputes and wished their members were somewhat less conscientious about discovering motes in their neighbors' eyes. But the quarrels had to be settled, and Backus took the task seriously.

On the other hand, the churches could prevent disputes from entering into the long and costly process of civil lawsuits. In most Baptist churches it was an article of faith and practice that "Brother ought not to go to Law with Brother but all matters of a legal nature between Brethren ought to be settled in the Church." Backus served on many councils which judged fine points of civil law according to principles of Christian equity—merchants accused of price-gouging their brethren; contracts unfulfilled or loans unrepaid; alleged thefts of a horse or cow; assault and battery; the mistreatment or misconduct of an apprentice. One of the more common causes of contention in later years was the repayment of old debts in depreciated paper money, which the civil law upheld in terms of the face value of the paper; the pietists always insisted that the debtor must repay full value.

Sometimes the disputes concerned matters of theology and doctrine. A pastor was accused of departing in his sermons from the proper Calvinistic interpretations of Scripture. A church member developed a heretical notion concerning salvation or election. Toward the end of the eighteenth century there was an increasing tendency to mitigate the harsher aspects of the famous Five Points of Calvinism, and Backus, who never departed from strict Calvinism, had the unhappy task of excommunicating many for the sin of Arminianism after 1770. Even some of the most noted Baptist pastors and revivalists "warped off" into the heresies of Universalism, Shakerism, and Methodism. Nevertheless, by the time these sects began to compete, the Baptists were too solidly established to be seriously shaken.

There is no precise way to measure the number of persons who joined the denomination after 1740; but it is possible, by using data which Backus himself carefully compiled, to measure the growth of the number of Baptist churches. In all of New England, including Rhode Island, there were thirty-three (of all Baptist varieties) in 1740. By 1777 Backus was able to name one hundred and nineteen closed-communion Calvinist churches; by 1784, one hundred and fifty-one; by 1795, three hundred and twenty-five. Making rough estimates for members (the number of actual baptized communicants), there may have been fifteen hundred Baptists in New England in 1740, six thousand in 1777, eight thousand in 1784, and 21,000 in 1795. For the number who professed Baptist principles, these figures could be multiplied by three. Backus, writing in 1786, estimated that since 1740 "above forty thousand people in New England have withdrawn from [the Standing Order] and the most of them have turned to the baptist denomination."

Backus was of course only one of many itinerants and evangelists who traveled the dirt roads and forest paths from one town to another year in and year out after 1740. Moreover, the movement had its own momentum quite apart from the efforts of these evangelists, in the spread of New Light ideas and the breakdown of the old Puritan traditions within the parishes. George Whitefield's evangelistic tours also helped to keep the New Light movement alive, and from its continued pietistic fervor the Baptists reaped the greatest gains. In addition, the increasing migration to northern and western frontiers included more than a fair proportion of Separates and Separate-Baptists persecuted in the older areas by religious taxes or seeking cheap and virgin land; come-outers in America have always been go-outers. On the freer and more tolerant frontier, where the old township and parish system broke down and the learned clergy were seldom seen, the pietism of the Baptists found fertile soil and rich harvests.

However, while the basic drive for expanding the Separate-Baptist movement was indigenous and most of its elders and evangelists were born and bred in New England, one group from outside that region played an extremely important part in the growth and stabilization of the denomination. These were the Baptist ministers from the Middle Colonies—notably from Philadelphia and New Jersey—who were sent or encouraged to go north by the Philadelphia Baptist Association after 1762. The most important of these men were James Manning; his brother-in-law, Hezekiah Smith; Samuel Stillman; and John Davis.

Most of these men were college-educated and therefore brought with them prestige and the capacity for leadership greatly needed. They were also the leading figures in founding Rhode Island College (later Brown University) and the Warren Baptist Association, the two institutions which provided the Baptist movement in New England with cohesion, status, and power. Coming when they did (the college in 1764 and the Warren Association in 1767), they caught the new movement at flood tide and helped to drive it over the banks without dissipating its energies. Above all they provided the basis for sustained attacks upon the New England establishment which did much to improve the position of the Baptists within the community and eventually put an end to compulsory religious taxation and the parish system.

Isaac Backus played no part in the founding of Brown University, though he did become a member of its first board of trustees in 1765. The idea for a college originated with Morgan Edwards, pastor of the First Baptist Church of Philadelphia, who, in 1762, brought it before the local Baptist Association for consideration. Initially it was thought that the basis for the college would be Isaac Eaton's academy in Hopewell, New Jersey, where many Baptists had prepared for Princeton. But New Jersey already had chartered a college for the Presbyterians at Princeton in 1746 and was considering another for the Dutch Reformed Calvinists at New Brunswick (granted in 1766), and the committee appointed to investigate the possibility suggested instead that consideration be given to establishing the college in Rhode Island, which had no college at all. In the summer of 1763, James Manning, on his way to Nova Scotia, stopped off in Newport to consult with some of the leading Baptists in that wealthy commercial community.

Since Backus had no friends in Newport (though there were three Baptist churches there) and had, in fact, never even visited the city, it was not surprising that he heard nothing of Manning's visit. Moreover, the college was conceived of as a Rhode Island project. The charter of a college was considered a public franchise designed, as was any public corporation, for the general welfare of the community. In return for their investment the incorporators expected to obtain a monopoly of that commodity or service they offered.

Ezra Stiles, the leading intellectual in Newport, was asked to draw up the proposal even though he was a Congregational minister. Stiles assumed that the college would be for the general public and not specifically for the Baptists, and drafted a charter which gave control to no one denomination. The Baptists, however, thought he intentionally gave too much power to Congregationalists; and since the Quakers and the Baptists dominated the legislature, they rejected the proposal. In March, 1764, a new Charter gave complete control of the college to the Baptists, though Quakers, Congregationalists, and Episcopalians were specifically included among its trustees. The charter stated that "Absolute and uninterrupted Liberty of Conscience" shall be enjoyed by all members of the college and "youths of all Religious Denominations shall and may be freely admitted . . . and that the Sectarian differences of opinions shall not make any part of the Public and Classical Instruction" at the college.

The first full meeting of the corporation of the college in September, 1765, chose James Manning President and named Backus a trustee. Backus had first met Manning in October, 1764, and took an immediate liking to the younger man. "The more I get acquainted with Mr. Manning the more I esteem him both for his own temper and for his gift in opening the clear doctrine of the gospel." Manning, who was born in Elizabethtown, New Jersey, in 1738, had graduated from Princeton in 1762, and was a man of sound judgment and great administrative ability. As president of the college until his death in 1791, he provided a firm basis for its future growth. Though he was not a brilliant scholar or preacher and his publications were all ephemeral, the Baptists of New England owed him a great debt for his skill and perseverance. While the legislature granted the college the right to conduct several lotteries to raise money, it offered no direct financial assistance beyond a tax exemption on faculty property. Except for the generous donations of the Brown family of Providence, all of the financial support came from the fees of the students and the small subscriptions collected by traveling ministers soliciting for the college in England and throughout America.

Nothing could have been better calculated to overcome the prejudices of New England Puritans against the denomination than this evidence of its determination to create a learned ministry. However, many of the Separate-Baptists were at first hostile toward the college for this very reason. Backus noted a general suspicion of the enterprise among the rural ministers; and one prominent elder, Thomas Green of Leicester, said in 1766 to a friend of Backus, "Elder Backus's concern in the College with ye views he undertook it, appears to me plausable enough; yet I cannot see how he, acting faithfully upon his own declared principles [that a learned ministry tends toward an unconverted ministry] can long keep his standing as a member of that body; the chief of whose principles and views differing so widely from his. Perhaps he is to have the great blessing of being cast out for truth sake and so leave a Testimony behind him."

Eventually Manning won over all but a very few of the Baptists to belief in the value of a college. They had always felt ill at ease sending their children to Harvard or Yale, especially after the Awakening, and they were happy to be able to send their sons to an institution where they would not lose their faith. Manning always told his graduating classes that it was more important to be a converted than a learned minister, though it was better to be both. When Manning died, the distinguished Harvard-educated minister of Salem, Massachusetts, William Bentley, a man who had nothing but contempt for most Baptists (including Backus, Stillman, and Hezekiah Smith) said of Manning that he "possessed a fine person & was entitled to the public esteem."

The college graduated seven men in its first class in

1769. It averaged about ten graduates a year until the end of the century. But comparatively few of its total of 323 graduates by 1800 entered the ministry, and only a score of the more than 300 Baptist churches in New England in 1800 had learned preachers. Nevertheless the college provided many intangible benefits by lending morale and prestige to the movement. Backus served on its board for thirty-five years, faithfully attending every corporation meeting, helping to solicit funds, donating his own money and books, and, most important, overcoming the prejudices of rural Baptists against it.

Manning was also directly responsible for the founding of the Warren Baptist Association, which was of even greater importance than the college for the advancement of the new reformation. Backus was consulted by Manning in the early stage of planning and eventually played a very important role in persuading his Separate-Baptist brethren to join it. But being himself a pietist with all of the anti-institutional and anti-hierarchical feelings of the type, and having seen at firsthand in Connecticut the dangers to congregational autonomy from associations, consociations, and presbyteries, Backus was at first very cool toward the plan. He did attend the first meeting in Warren, Rhode Island, in September, 1767, to which Manning had called three Philadelphians who could explain how effectively their association had aided the Baptists in the Middle Colonies. They sustained Manning's claims that the system of associations was an old one among Baptists, that it had worked well in the Middle Colonies since 1707, and that it gave unity and strength to the denomination without in any way infringing upon the rights of the individual churches. Manning then read to the delegates a plan of organization which was virtually a duplicate of that of the Philadelphia Association.

The constitution began by asserting that "some of the

uses" of such an association were "union and communion"
among the member churches; "maintaining more effectually the order and faith once delivered to the saints;
having advice in cases of doubt, and help in distress; being
more able to promote the good of the cause, and becoming
important in the eye of the civil powers"—the last a reference to the combat against the ecclesiastical laws of New
England. Next the constitution described the procedures
for admission and for the choice of delegates to the annual
meetings. It concluded by limiting membership to those
closed-communion Calvinistic Baptists who subscribed to
the confession of faith adopted by the Calvinistic Baptists of
Great Britain in the year 1689. In particular it required
members to believe in the following doctrines: "The im-
putation of Adam's sin to his posterity; the inability of
man to recover himself; effectual calling by Sovereign
grace; justification by imputed righteousness; immersion
for baptism and that on profession of faith and repentance; congregational churches and their independency;
reception into them upon evidence of sound conversion."

While there was no quarrel among any of the delegates
about the doctrinal basis of the association, there was considerable dispute over its power to settle quarrels within
or among the member churches. Backus was one of the
most forthright in objecting that the association might set
itself up as a presbytery to control the churches. Manning
insisted that the constitution gave the association only advisory not compulsory power; and that the plan had
worked for sixty years in Philadelphia without in any way
restricting the autonomy of the churches. After several
days of argument, however, only four churches were willing to join, and Backus's was not one of them.

Backus objected to the clause in the constitution which
stated that whenever a dispute came to it for settlement
the association would search the Bible for a text applicable

to the situation. Votes were to be called for only when no such text was found. Backus pointed out that the resort to Scripture required skilled exegesis and that the association would thus turn over all its power to a few learned men.

Other Separate-Baptists voiced similar objections, insisting that the association "supports a classical government over the churches of Christ" and would thereby "over throw the independence of the churches of Christ." Manning twice rewrote the constitution, changing the disputed clause to read simply "All matters [are] to be determined in this Association by the suffrage of the messengers, except what are determinable by Scripture," and emphasizing "That such an association is consistent with the independency and power of particular churches because it pretends to no other than an advisory council, utterly disclaiming superiority, jurisdiction, coercive right and infallibility."

This finally convinced Backus and the majority of the Separate-Baptists, and thereafter new churches joined the association almost as rapidly as they were formed. By 1780 it had thirty-eight members, most of them from Massachusetts. A second Baptist association was formed in 1772 to serve Connecticut. The New Hampshire Association was formed in 1776; the Shaftesbury Association was formed in 1780 and the Woodstock Association (serving Vermont and eastern New York) in 1781. By 1804 there were thirteen Baptist associations in New England with 312 churches and 23,638 communicants.

With the formation of the Warren Association, the Baptist movement in New England entered a period of rapid growth and consolidation. The Association served as an arena in which common problems could be adjudicated and common stands taken on controversial problems of doctrine, practice, and discipline. Messengers from other

associations attended each others' meetings to maintain
communications and unity among them all. The associations promoted peace and harmony by refusing to admit
churches which could not settle their quarrels among themselves or with their neighbors, by disapproving of schisms
on frivolous or non-essential points, by formal pronounce-
ments upon doctrinal issues, and by warning the denomination against new heresies. The Warren Association (and
later the other associations) urged upon Baptists the importance of giving their pastors adequate salaries; it
warned them against disorderly itinerants; and it emphasized the importance of family prayers. But in all of
these actions it scrupulously avoided interfering with local
autonomy. It refused to adjudicate quarrels within individual churches or between member churches—leaving
these to *ad hoc* councils. It did on occasion expel a
church which failed to adhere to the constitutional practices of the association and it refused admission to some,
but such cases were few and limited to such flagrant mal-
feasance as aroused no objections.

Perhaps its most useful functions were in promoting ex-
pansion by providing pastors to supply vacant churches,
by ordaining traveling evangelists, by publishing membership statistics, by encouraging the formation of new
associations, and by pastoral and circulating letters published in the minutes each year which exhorted the Baptists to go forward in their new reformation. It called for
annual days of fasting and prayer relating to specific tribu-
lations of their own denomination. It solicited contributions for the support of the college. And in 1769 it encouraged Backus to begin collecting materials for a history
of the Baptists in New England—a piece of propaganda
which would set the record straight and correct the many
prejudices against the denomination in previous accounts,
all written by Puritan ministers.

Of all the activities which the Warren Association undertook to strengthen and advance the Baptist movement, none was more effective and important than the unity it gave to efforts to obtain release from compulsory religious taxation. Two years after its founding, in 1769, the association voted to create a Grievance Committee charged with the immediate task of petitioning the legislature for religious liberty. As its secondary task, this committee was instructed to act as the center for collecting all instances of "persecution" by the various towns and parishes of any individual Baptist or Baptist church. Backus became a key member of this committee even before his church had joined the association. And after 1770 he devoted an increasing amount of his time and energy to it. Within a very short space of time he became the principal spokesman for the Baptists in their efforts to disestablish the Puritan churches. As such he did more than any other man to formulate and publicize the evangelical position on Church and State which was ultimately to prevail throughout America.

V

The Grievance Committee and the Revolution
1769–1775

"No one whose bosom feels the patriot glow in behalf of civil liberty can remain torpid to the more ennobling flame of RELIGIOUS FREEDOM.*"* Baptist Memorial to the Continental Congress, 1774.

UNTIL 1769 Backus and the Separate-Baptists were too busy stabilizing their denomination to devote sustained effort to the question of religious liberty. They had many times protested locally against compulsory taxation, and in 1748 and 1754 had petitioned the Massachusetts and Connecticut General Assemblies in vain for repeal of the laws requiring religious taxes, or at least for exemption of Baptists. Fatalistic resignation led the Separate-Baptists to concentrate their efforts upon evangelistic soul winning. There seemed no effective way to force the majority to alter its ecclesiastical system.

In those years the Separate-Baptists were more concerned with defects in the exemption laws than with complete separation of Church and State. Had the existing system been impartially applied, they might, like the Quakers, have lapsed into pragmatic acquiescence. Because the efforts of the Puritans to grant religious liberty to dissenters after 1727 did not prove workable, the Baptists continued to fight.

After 1769 the struggle entered a new and far more aggressive phase, simultaneous with the revolutionary efforts of the colonies against political oppression from England. In both struggles Backus played a leading intellectual and practical role. He wrote several important tracts; he drew up dozens of petitions; he obtained factual evidence of persecution for propagandistic and legal purposes; he appeared in court as a witness; he worked on committees to formulate and execute policies; and he carried on a constant warfare of words in the newspapers, public disputes, and private letters. His own sufferings from religious persecution, the imprisonment of his mother, brother, and uncle in Connecticut, and his deep pietistic convictions produced in him a passionate and unrelenting opposition to the established system. With the formation of the Warren Association and its Grievance Committee he at last possessed the resources he needed to crusade for the downfall of this system.

At the annual meeting of the Warren Baptist Association in 1769, Backus recorded in its minutes as scribe of the meeting, "Many of the letters from the Churches [in the association] mentioned grievous oppressions and persecutions from the 'Standing Order,' especially the church from Ashfield where religious tyranny had been carried to great lengths. Wherefor John Davis, Henry Williams, Isaac Backus, Richard Montague, John Fulsham, and Ebenezer Davis, were appointed a Committee to prepare petitions to the General Courts of Massachusetts and Connecticut for redress." In addition the assembled delegates voted a plan to "collect Grievances" and formally declared war against the Standing Order. The association appointed a committee "to pursue this resolution by petition and memorial," even to the King if need be. Isaac Backus, Samuel Stillman, Hezekiah Smith, Richard Montague, Joseph Meacham, and Thomas Whitman were "to receive all attested grievances" which would serve as the basis for the petition to the King.

One of the college-educated "western brethren" from New Jersey, John Davis, soon to become pastor of the Second Baptist Church of Boston, was chairman of this Grievance Committee. For three years he pursued a vigorous and effective course of action which gave impressive impetus to the movement for disestablishment. Davis had been born in the Welsh Tract, New Castle County, Delaware, in 1737. Son of a Baptist minister, Davis studied at the academy of Isaac Eaton and graduated in 1763 from the College of Philadelphia. He taught school for several years in Newark, New Jersey, and engaged in mathematical research which earned him admission to the American Philosophical Society in the summer of 1768. That same year he was elected a Fellow of the new Baptist college in Rhode Island and a year later he came to New England to look for a pastorate. In 1769 he was preaching on trial at the Second Baptist Church in Boston and a year later he was formally ordained as its pastor.

Davis's first task, and that of the committee, was to come to the aid of the Ashfield Baptists whose letter had led to the creation of the Grievance Committee. The Ashfield case raised difficult issues connected with the gradual evolution of the Massachusetts laws in regard to the rights of dissenters. The first law exempting Baptists and Quakers from religious taxes, passed in 1728, stated that "none of the persons commonly called Anabaptists, nor any of those commonly called Quakers" who alleged "a scruple of conscience as the reason for their refusal to pay" religious taxes should henceforth pay a poll tax toward the support of the Standing Order "provided that such persons do usually attend the meetings of their respective Societies assembling upon the Lord's Day for the worship of God, and that they live within five miles of the place of such meeting." A year later an amendment excluded the property as well as the polls of Anabaptists and Quakers, thereby giving them complete exemption. But the problem was to define who were Anabaptists and Quakers and how they could compel the assessors to grant them exemption. In many towns either the law was ignored or else many who claimed to be Anabaptists or Quakers were nonetheless taxed by assessors who believed that they were only tax dodgers.

In 1734 a new law aimed to make "better known what persons are of that persuasion" and therefore exempt. The assessors were required to "take a list of all such persons" by July 20 of each year and to "transmit the same to the clerk of the town" to be entered on the town records "so any of the people called Anabaptists or any member of their Society thereto appointed may view such list. . . . and if any person of that denomination shall be omitted in such list. . . . and the assessors shall be certified thereof in writing, under the hands of two principal members of that persuasion" prior to September 10, then these names would be added. However, the "two principal members" of each dissenting congregation who added names to the original list had to certify that they believed such persons "to be conscientiously of their persuasion and that they do frequently and usually attend their meetings for the worship of God on the Lord's Day." This amendment to the law also eliminated the requirement that a dissenter had to live within five miles of the church or society to which he belonged.

The Quakers, who received similar exemption, found

these terms entirely to their satisfaction and thereafter played no part in the movement to disestablish the Puritan churches. The Old Baptists also seemed content, and the law was renewed in 1740 and in 1747. The renewal in 1747 indicates that at that time the Separate-Baptist movement had not yet made itself felt, and the legislature merely understood that it was renewing the privileges of the Old Baptists.

By 1753, however, the Separate-Baptist movement had created new complications, when its churches claimed the privilege of tax exemption. The legislature, at the request of the delegates from towns where the Separate-Baptists were becoming numerous and vociferous, decided to clarify the situation by enacting a more stringent act, expressly designed to exclude the Separate-Baptists from exemption by making it difficult, if not impossible, for them to obtain certification.

Since "many doubts" had arisen about the status of these Baptists, said the act, and "in many cases the said exemption has been extended to many persons to whom the same was never designed to extend," new terms were necessary "in order to ascertain more effectually what persons shall be esteemed and accounted as Anabaptist, and to whom the said exemption shall thereafter be extended." It required all groups claiming exemption as Baptists to obtain certification from the Old Baptist churches: "no minister nor members of any Anabaptist Church . . . shall be esteemed qualified to give such certificate . . . other than such as shall have obtained from three other churches commonly called Anabaptists, in this or the neighboring Provinces, a certificate from each respectively, that they esteem such church to be one of their denomination."

The act was designed to crush the Separate-Baptist movement, for the Old Baptists were not in fellowship with the new ones. The Old Baptists were Arminians, opposed to the Awakening and to the Calvinistic, "free grace" views of the Separate-Baptists, and would not conscientiously certify their churches as bona fide Baptist churches. But the law did not work out as intended. There was no way of specifying which Baptist churches had the right to certify others. The Separate-Baptists simply certified each other. The act was troublesome, however, and if the town or parish wanted to question the process of certification, the Baptists were obliged to take the matter into court for a long adjudication before judges and jurors who were rarely inclined in their favor.

This act remained in force for five years and was renewed in 1758 for three more years. When the Grievance Committee was formed, the law had again been renewed (in 1761) for ten years more.

Another aspect to the exemption of dissenters was even more directly related to the Baptists in Ashfield. The exemption acts provided that no dissenter was to be exempted from religious taxes in a newly settled plantation until it had built a meeting-house and settled an "able, learned, and orthodox" minister. This clause lay at the root of the complaints from Ashfield.

Among the first settlers of Ashfield (founded in 1736) were Chileab Smith and his family. Smith had been converted in the Great Awakening, joined the parish church in Hadley, separated from it, and shortly thereafter, in 1739 or 1740 moved to Ashfield. Since there was no church, he began exercising his spiritual gifts as a New Light exhorter in meetings for his family and neighbors. Eventually, he and his followers adopted antipedobaptist views and were immersed on June 27, 1761. A month later they formed a Baptist church and ordained Chileab Smith's son Ebenezer as their pastor. Probably the majority of the inhabitants of the town were Baptists, and they decided to build a meetinghouse. Thereupon the nonresident proprietors, who own most of the land in the town, became alarmed. Baptist control would drive down the value of the land and ruin their speculative hopes. Respectable people would not live in a town where the Baptists had a majority and where, consequently, taxes for the Standing Church would be sky high on the Congregational minority.

When Ebenezer Smith claimed exemption from civil taxes as the settled minister of the plantation, the courts denied his claim because he lacked a college degree or its equivalent. The proprietors then hired a Yale graduate, the Rev. Jacob Sherwin, who formed a church; with the influx of new settlers the Congregationalists soon outnumbered the Baptists. The proprietors then laid taxes for the erection of a meetinghouse and for the support of Mr. Sherwin, as they were obliged to do by law, and the Baptists had no choice but to submit. They had to abandon building their own meetinghouse since they did not have enough money to pay for it as well.

In 1765 the plantation was incorporated as a town. Technically at that moment the Baptists ceased to be responsible for paying religious taxes and came under the exemption act. Nevertheless the town continued to tax them on the grounds that the meetinghouse was not yet completed. The Baptists paid under protest for three years and then petitioned the legislature, which sympathized with them until Israel Williams, one of the chief proprietors and most important political figures in western Massachusetts, pointed out that Smith and his group were really Separates or New Light fanatics and not entitled to exemption as Baptists. At his urging the legislature passed in June, 1768, the "Ashfield Law" which the Baptists maintained was unconstitutional. It required all the inhabitants of Ashfield to support Sherwin and the Standing Church despite the general exemption statutes. A petition for relief in 1769 was dismissed. The town proceeded to levy taxes upon the Baptists. They refused to pay. The constables thereupon sold their land in a deliberate effort to drive them out of town.

At this point the Grievance Committee went into action. John Davis visited Ashfield and in June, 1770, assisted Ebenezer Smith in presenting a new but futile petition to the legislature. The Warren Association at its meeting in September of that year appointed a new Grievance Committee and "Rev. Hezekiah Smith was chosen Agent to the Court of Great Britain to act in conjunction with Rev. Dr. Samuel Stennet[t] and Thomas Llewelyn, L.B.D. of London," two prominent Baptist leaders, to petition the King. The committee then decided to make one more petition to the General Assembly protesting that as a result of the Ashfield Law "398 acres of our land have been sold to build and remove and repair when moved a meeting-house in which we have no part. . . . The lands were valued at three hundred and sixty-three pounds thirteen shillings, lawful money, and were sold for nineteen pounds fifteen shillings, lawful money. . . . Part of said lands had been laid out for a burying place and they have taken from us our dead. They have also sold a dwelling-house and orchard and pulled up our apple trees and thrown down our fences and made our fields waste places."

The hoped-for repeal of the Ashfield Law did not come, though the legislature passed a new and milder tax exemption law which went into effect on January 31, 1771. The old pejorative term "Anabaptists" which the Baptists hated, was replaced by "Antipedobaptists" to designate the denomination. Exemption from religious taxation applied to all members of Baptist congregations and not just to converted, immersed members of the churches. The certificate of membership did not require the signature of the minister if the church was temporarily without one. And any parish or town could, by majority vote, exempt all dissenters from religious taxes permanently and thus put an end to certification. But these concessions did not mollify the Baptists. Since the Ashfield Law remained in effect, religious taxes continued to be laid upon the Baptists there and their lands continued to be sold. The Grievance Committee could wait no longer to seek disallowance of the law by the King; an act not disallowed within three years after passage was automatically approved. Lieutenant Governor Thomas Hutchinson, who had no love for the rebellious General Assembly and who undoubtedly saw a chance here to drive a wedge into the Massachusetts community by exacerbating the religious quarrel, advised the Baptists to carry their appeal to the Crown.

The Baptists were well aware that they would only add to the resentment against them if they turned to the King for help while other colonists were challenging the royal authority. A letter in one of the Boston newspapers had already accused John Davis of being "very much suspect" as "one employed by the enemies of America to defame and blacken the Colonies." Nevertheless the Baptists appealed to the King, though several of their most prominent members did not concur. The Reverend Samuel Stennett, pastor of the Calvinistic Baptist Church in Little Wild Street in London and an influential person at the court of George III, presented a petition to the Lord Commissioners of Trade and Plantations in June, 1771, "on behalf of the Baptists in Ashfield." The Commissioners approved and on July 31, 1771, the King disallowed the Ashfield Law. The news reached Massachusetts in October. It was a long while before the legal tangles were unsnarled, however, and the Ashfield Baptists claimed they never did get back all that was rightfully due to them.

Backus's part in the Ashfield affair established him as

the most hard-working member of the Grievance Committee. He favored pressing the matter to the King; and he assisted Davis in drawing up the petitions, consulted at length with Chileab Smith and his son Ebenezer, and wrote two tracts calling upon the legislature to grant more religious liberty to the Baptists. Consequently when John Davis became ill in the spring of 1772 and left New England for warmer climes in July, Backus was chosen to take his place as "The agent for the Baptists in New England" and the chairman of the Grievance Committee of the Warren Association.

The Ashfield victory by no means solved the general problems of tax exemption. In August, 1770, the Grievance Committee had placed an advertisement in the Boston *Evening Post*, asking "The Baptists in the Province of Massachusetts Bay who are or have been oppressed in any way on a religious account" to collect and transmit "cases of suffering and have them well attested—such as the taxes you have paid to build meeting-houses, to settle ministers, and support them, with all the time, money, and labour you have lost in waiting on courts, seeing lawyers, etc." Among Backus's papers are dozens of these affidavits and letters from all over the province which added up to clear proof that the exemption act was being unjustly administered, to the injury of the Baptists.

Assessors refused to accept the certificates of persons who were members of the congregation but not of the church. Certificates were invalidated for minor infractions; many Baptists were taxed and distrained because they turned in their certificates a day or two late or because they did not follow precisely the wording set forth in the law. Baptists taxed despite valid certificates were frustrated in the courts, which ruled that they should have brought suit against assessors instead of against the tax collector, or vice versa. A man in Chelmsford, on the ad-

vice of a Congregational lawyer, brought suit against both
the assessors and the collector in 1773 only to find when
he won his case against one that the damages he had to pay
for falsely suing the other were higher than those he received. Moreover, in any case which a Baptist won the
town indemnified its agent and voted a tax upon all its
inhabitants (including the Baptists) to pay the fine levied
against him by the court. The most common complaint
was against towns which invalidated certificates on the
ground that the Baptists were really Separates. The law
seemed so obviously weighted against the Baptists that
often it was easier to pay the tax or allow their property
to be distrained. Many complained that the courts and
juries, made up almost wholly of Congregationalists, were
prejudiced.

Backus had to deal at firsthand with all of these cases.
His experience year after year made him extremely pes-
simistic about the attitude of the Congregationalists. Even
laws equitable in their wording were not administered
impartially by the local authorities. Local assessors, collectors, and constables deliberately flouted the law out
of prejudice. Courts tolerated this petty harassment by
frequently using technicalities against the Baptists but
seldom against their oppressors.

The Baptists finally reached the point of exasperation
in 1773, a year which Backus considered a turning point in
his own life as well as in the movement itself. The Baptists then decided to adopt a policy of massive civil disobedience to assert their rights of conscience. They had ex-
hausted all of the lawful means of redress for their grievances and had patiently borne a long train of abuses; now
they had no choice but to stand up and fight by unlawful
means. The new step was taken by the Grievance Committee on May 5, 1773, at a meeting in Boston.

Backus printed the decision in a letter to all of the Baptist churches in the association. The letter called attention to new persecutions in Mendon and Chelmsford. "Liberty of conscience, the great and most important article of liberty, is evidently not allowed as it ought to be in this country, not even by the very men who are now making loud complaints of encroachments upon their own liberties [by Parliament]." The "root of all these difficulties," was the assumption by civil rulers of a power to govern ecclesiastical affairs or to use "force to support ministers." No connection between Church and State was justifiable if it limited the freedom of "ecclesiastical affairs." The Baptists were no longer content to act within the prevailing system, to accept a policy of mere toleration. They wanted religious liberty as a general principle, as a natural right, and not a denominational privilege.

The Grievance Committee had decided that it was a "duty to strike so directly at this root, as to refuse any conformity to their laws about such affairs, even so much as giving any certificates to their assessors." If all of them refused thereafter to pay any religious taxes, and if the collectors were thus forced to imprison or distrain every Baptist in the province, that would expose the enormity of the problem and the intensity of their conviction. The costs might at first be great in money and suffering, but "We are fully persuaded that if we were all united in bearing what others of our friends might, for a little while, suffer on this account, a less sum than has already been expended with lawyers and courts on such accounts would carry us through the trial." The Standing Order, seeing how determined the Baptists were and with what "a christian temper" they bore any sufferings inflicted during this period of massive civil disobedience, would feel obliged to change their system because it would "appear so odious" to them.

Backus and the Baptists had the example of the radical

action of their compatriots in defying the unjust laws of
Britain. The letter made this explicit. Three years earlier
Backus, in a tract entitled *A Seasonable Plea for Liberty of
Conscience Against Some Late Oppressive Proceedings
Particularly in the Town of Berwick* (Boston, 1770), had
pointed out that "many who are filling the nation with the
cry of LIBERTY and against oppressors [in Parliament]
are at the same time themselves violating the dearest of all
rights, LIBERTY OF CONSCIENCE." He quoted John
Locke's *Letters on Toleration* to prove the natural right
not only of life, liberty, and property but also of conscience.
Liberty of conscience was not simply a right of English-
men but one of "the rights of mankind." The Standing
ministers were vehemently exclaiming "against the scheme
of imposing episcopacy upon them, while the same persons impose cruelly upon their neighbors" in religious
affairs. Backus, however, by no means identified liberty
with government by the majority, for it was the tyranny
of the majority in New England which denied the rights of
the Baptists. Like a true pietist, he placed as much reliance
upon Biblical texts as upon the works of Locke to prove
the necessity for separation of Church and State.

When the Grievance Committee met with the Warren
Association at Medfield in September, 1773, Backus did
not find it easy to convince all of his brethren to adopt the
course of civil disobedience. "Some doubted the expediency of our now refusing any compliance with their laws
in that respect." A compromise measure which permitted
each church to make its own individual decision greatly
weakened the effort. For despite the fact that there were
"thirty-four elders and brethren against giving any more
certificates" and only "six for it and three at a loss how to
act," when the matter was left up to each individual church
there was considerably less unanimity. The failure of the

association to follow Backus's recommendation dissipated the zeal which would have resulted from solid denominational unity. The association did vote, however, that united denominational support would be given to raise funds on behalf of any persons who suffered as the result of the refusal to turn in certificates. The Warren Association also instructed Backus to publish, in its name, a tract of sixty-two pages, part of which he had read to the association, in defense of civil disobedience.

An Appeal to the Public for Religious Liberty Against the Oppression of the Present Day (1773) was the most important of the thirty-seven tracts which Backus published during his lifetime and was central to the whole movement for separation of Church and State in America. It remains the best exposition of the eighteenth century pietistic concept of separation.

Basic to the Baptist position was the belief that all direct connections between the state and institutionalized religion must be broken in order that America might become a truly Christian country. Backus, like Jefferson and Madison, believed that "Truth is great and will prevail"—but by "Truth" he meant the revealed doctrines of grace. His fundamental assumption was that "God has appointed two different kinds of government in the world which are different in their nature and ought never to be confounded together; one of which is called civil, the other ecclesiastical government." The two had been "confounded together" by the Emperor Constantine and the Papacy and had ultimately been brought to New England by the Puritans "who had not taken up the cross so as to separate from the national church before they came away." A "Brief view of how civil and ecclesiastical affairs are blended together among us [in 1773] to the depriving of many of God's people of that liberty of conscience which he [God] has given us" utilized also the long-forgotten arguments of Roger Williams to defend the doctrines of separation.

Backus defined three encroachments upon religious liberty imbedded in the ecclesiastical system of Massachusetts: The legislature compelled every parish to support "a pedobaptist worship . . . although it is well known that infant baptism is never express'd in the Bible." The legislature compelled men to have "either an academical degree or a testimonial in his favour from a majority of the ministers in the county" before they could be ordained; thus Christ's gifts were restrained by men's laws. Above all, God clearly stated that ministers were to be supported voluntarily by the freewill gifts of their auditors and not by compulsion. A Christian commonwealth had to abandon practices contrary to the gospel. "Now who can hear Christ declare that his kingdom is NOT OF THIS WORLD, and yet believe that this blending of the church and state together can be pleasing to him?"

Backus mentioned also the flaw in the ecclesiastical system which ultimately proved its downfall. His pietistic sensitivity to heresy already had detected the trend toward Unitarianism at Harvard which the New Lights within the Standing Order ignored for the sake of stability and order. The requirement of a learned pedobaptist ministry being considered primary, questions of theology and orthodoxy were secondary. "Indeed as to doctrine, ministers who preach differently, yea, directly contrary to each other about Christ and his salvation, yet are supported by these laws which at the same time limit the people to one circumstantial mode [regarding baptism]." A man of Arminian or Unitarian tendencies from Harvard received the legal backing of the state while a sound

Calvinist who would not baptize infants was declared in-
competent.

Backus touched upon the arguments of natural rights
and charter privileges in the tract, but only tangentially.
He refuted the argument set forth in defense of the Ashfield Law that "Natural rights" were "wholly superceded
in this case by civil obligations": the safety and good order
of the state required the limitation upon the right of religious liberty; and in entering the social compact the
Baptists, like all other men, yielded that much of their
natural rights as was needed to support a Christian commonwealth. Backus's answer revealed his sensitivity to the
charge that a voluntaristic, individualistic system of religion would lead to the decay of Christian worship and
reduce the commonwealth to a state of barbarism. The
Baptists of Ashfield had not pleaded for natural rights
and they did not wish society "restored to a state of
nature." Their arguments rested on "Charter privilege."

Backus did, however, stress the theory of natural rights
in regard to property. The Baptists could rightly make
the same claim as the American colonists against Parliament, that they were being taxed without representation.
"Our civil legislature" are not "our representatives in
religious affairs." They were elected as representatives for
civil or secular affairs only, and when they acted in ecclesiastical affairs, they meddled in matters upon which
their constituents did not empower them to legislate.
"Religion is a voluntary obedience unto God which therefore force cannot promote." The Baptist who was forced
to support a worship he could not attend in conscience
was deprived of his property without his consent; and
presumably even a Congregationalist could not, if he
chose, authorize his representative to make ecclesiastical
laws. "You do not deny the right of the British parliament

to impose taxes within her own realm; only complain that she extends her taxing power beyond her proper limits; and have we not as good right to say you do the same thing?"

The tract was also full of examples of the ways in which the laws exempting the Baptists were ignored, perverted, or narrowly construed. He went out of his way to deny the charge that the Baptists, in resorting so often to law, were tax dodgers: "Many of us have expended ten or twenty times as much in setting up and supporting that worship which we believe to be right as it would have cost us to have continued in the fashionable way, yet we are often accused of being covetous."

As a pietist he rejected the argument that the majority should rule in religious affairs. The Massachusetts system persecuted minorities since the major vote of any parish chose the minister to whom all inhabitants had to pay taxes. The people of New England were not supporting religion by their system. The majority could not judge religious truth, particularly in a society where so few of the voters were truly converted. The law which gave "saints or sinners, believers or unbelievers" an equal vote in the choice of the parish minister was but the establishment of a secular state, the triumph of Satan over the true saints.

Backus concluded his tract by summing up in a numerical list the reasons why "We are therefore brought to a stop about paying so much regard to such laws as to give in annual certificates to the other denomination, as we have formerly done." Jefferson in his preamble to the Religious Liberty Act of Virginia and Madison in his famous Remonstrance of 1785 utilized essentially deistic arguments based upon reason and natural law. Backus's arguments were pure pietism. The Puritan establishment, he said, and the certificate laws were wrong

(1) because they acknowledged that "the civil power" had "a right to set one religious sect up above another."

(2) because the right to tax was a claim to the "right to govern in Christ's kingdom which is not of this world."

(3) because the established system emboldened people "to judge the liberty of other men's consciences."

(4) because "bringing in an earthly power between Christ and his people has been the grand source of anti-Christian abominations."

(5) because "by the law of Christ every man is not only allowed but also required to judge for himself concerning the circumstantials as well as the essentials of religion, and to act according to the full persuasion of his own mind." Coercive measures about religion provoked "emulation, wrath and contention." "Who can describe all the mischiefs of this nature that such measures have produced in our land!"

An Appeal to the Public was pietistic America's declaration of spiritual independence. Like Jefferson's Declaration three years later, it contained a legal brief against a long train of abuses, a theoretical defense of principle, and a moral argument for civil disobedience.

Meanwhile the Baptists who declined to give in any further certificates found their names put back upon the tax lists for the maintenance of public worship. When the arrest or distraint of several members of Backus's congregation who lived in Taunton seemed imminent on January 10, 1774, Backus wrote to Samuel Adams, now at the height of his influence as a Son of Liberty, urging him to speak out on behalf of religious freedom. Judge Peter Oliver, who had himself instructed the assessors in Taunton to tax the Baptists, was a Tory, notoriously opposed to the Sons of Liberty. Backus also reminded Adams that the exemption act of 1771 had expired and the question of its renewal or alteration would soon be before the legislature: "I hope, sir, that you will give proof both to the court and to the world, that you regard the religious as well as the civil rights of your countrymen." Without some remedial action a large number "of as peaceable people and as hearty friends to their country as any in the land" might "carry their complaints before those who would be glad to hear that the Legislature of Massachusetts deny to their fellow servants that liberty which they so earnestly insist upon for themselves. A word to the wise is sufficient." Sam Adams, however, was a staunch conservative in religious affairs and never displayed any sympathy for separation of Church and State.

The legislature, ignoring Backus's threats, merely voted to extend the expired exemption act for another three years. Now the Grievance Committee faced a difficult decision: whether to petition the King and thus embarrass the patriot cause just as it was reaching a new climax, thereby earning the wrath of their neighbors for disloyalty to the province, or to lose face with their own members by yielding.

The Sons of Liberty and Parliament provided a way out. In retaliation for the Boston Tea Party in December, 1773, Parliament passed the Coercive Acts in the spring of 1774, closing the port of Boston to trade and virtually annulling the Massachusetts charter. These acts, and the Quebec and Quartering Acts, led directly to the First Continental Congress which met in Philadelphia in September, 1774. Now the Baptists could appeal to a higher authority than the Massachusetts legislature, one which was created by the united colonies. The Baptists could thus at once prove their loyalty to the patriot cause and also seek redress of their grievances outside the province.

The notion of appealing to the Congress came from the "western brethren," who arrived in Providence in the first week of September to attend the annual commencement at the College. Stephen Gano of New York and William Van Horn of Pennsylvania suggested that Backus go to Philadelphia. They told him that "now was the most likely time to obtain our religious liberty that we had ever known. I had many objections against it, but when I awaked next morning, the religious liberties of three colonies, or more, appeared so weighty to my mind that if I might do anything for their relief, I was made willing to do it, and leave my private concerns to him that orders all things."

A week later the Warren Association directed Backus to go to Congress as the agent for the Baptists in New England and contributed £6.10.1 3/4 toward his expenses. Number seventeen of the Suffolk Resolves, passed by a convention in Suffolk County shortly before he set out, seemed so germane to his mission that he took a copy of the Resolves with him. This article read, "This county, confiding in the wisdom and integrity of the Continental Congress now sitting at Philadelphia, will pay all due respect and submission to such measures as may be recommended by them to the colonies for the restoration and establishment of our just rights, civil and religious."

James Manning went along and so did Chileab Smith of Ashfield—a living witness to the worst persecution of the sect. These three met at the home of Robert Strettle Jones, a prominent Philadelphia lawyer and a Baptist, who had helped to draw up the charter for Rhode Island College. Backus also found waiting for him in Jones's home three of the leading Quakers of Philadelphia, Israel and James Pemberton and Joseph Fox, who "manifested a willingness to be helpful."

The Pembertons and Fox were the leaders of one of the most important social, political, and economic groups in Pennsylvania. Men of great influence in the legislature, at this moment they were vitally concerned with the actions of the Continental Congress. No doubt it seemed that the joining together of the two dissenting groups in the petition to Congress would remove some of the stigma from the Baptists and make the effort seem less narrow and self-interested.

As it turned out, the decision proved to be a serious tactical mistake. Had the Baptists been more astute politically they would have considered the fact that the Philadelphia Quakers were not only pacifists but Loyalists who disliked the general movement toward independence. To Sam Adams, John Adams, Robert Treat Paine and the other New England delegates to the convention, the alliance with the Philadelphia Quakers only confirmed the old suspicion that the Baptists were Tory in their inclinations and enemies to the patriot cause. John Adams was "greatly surprised and somewhat indignant" when he found Israel Pemberton with the Baptist delegation—"A Quaker of large property and more intrigue" who was "endeavoring to avail himself of this opportunity to break up the Congress."

Backus and Manning were innocent dupes. There is some evidence, however, that "the western brethren," like Robert Strettle Jones, shared the Quakers' views toward the impending crisis. And Morgan Edwards, who had been a leading influence in the Philadelphia Association, had publicly stated his Tory sympathies in 1772.

The Quakers, said Backus, "advised us not to address the Congress as a body at present, but to seek for a conference with the Massachusetts delegates, together with some others who were known to be friends to religious liberty." A meeting on the evening of October 14 in Carpenters Hall was attended by the four delegates from Massachusetts, by Stephen Hopkins and Samuel Ward of Rhode Island, by Joseph Galloway and Thomas Miflin of Philadelphia, by James Kinsey of New Jersey, by Mayor Samuel Rhodes of Philadelphia, by the three Quakers, by seven or more members of the Philadelphia Baptist

Association, and by the delegates from the Warren Association—Backus, Manning, and Chileab Smith.

Manning opened the meeting by reading a long memorial which he and Backus and Robert Strettle Jones had drawn up. It pointed out that the Revolution was a fight for political and religious liberty. "The free exercise of private judgment and the unalienable rights of conscience," it explained, were "of too high a . . . dignity to be subjected to . . . the imperfect laws of fallible legislators. The merciful Father of mankind" was "alone Lord of Conscience" and liberty, virtue, and public happiness could be supported without establishments. The memorial went on to give a historical survey of the persecutions under the exemption acts of Massachusetts, with special emphasis on the Ashfield Case and on the fact that Baptists in new plantations were still required to pay to build the first Congregational meetinghouse and to support the installation of the first Congregational minister. Calling this an infringement of charter rights and contrary to the principles of "the great Mr. Locke," the memorial utilized Backus's argument that "the magistrate's power extends not to the establishing of any articles of faith or forms of worship by force of laws" and reasserted the pietistic justification of separation. Religion was "a concern between God and the soul with which no human authority can intermeddle." The Baptists claimed the liberty of worshipping God according to their consciences "as men, as Christians, and by charter as inhabitants of Massachusetts Bay."

As might be expected, John and Sam Adams rose to the defense of their province. As Backus recorded it in his diary, "John Adams made a long speech, and Samuel Adams another, both of whom said, 'There is indeed an ecclesiastical establishment in our province; but a very slender one, hardly to be called an establishment.'" They shifted their plea when Backus called attention to the persecution of Baptists and asserted that the "General Court was clear of blame" and had always been ready to hear complaints "whatever might have been done by executive officers [i.e., tax assessors and collectors]." Robert Treat Paine argued that much of the trouble "was due to the refusal of the Baptists to make themselves known by giving in certificates." It was suggested that the Baptists' real complaint had nothing to do with liberty of conscience but was "only a contending about paying a little money." To this charge Backus rose angrily to assert, "It is absolutely a point of conscience with me; for I cannot give in the certificates they require without implicitly acknowledging that power in man which I believe belongs to God."

The conference ended without any alteration of opinions. The Massachusetts delegates promised "to do what they could" but it was evident that they would do very little. John Adams told Backus, "We might as soon expect a change in the solar system as to expect that they would give up their establishment."

Backus did not report in his diary anything said by the Quakers at this meeting, an indication perhaps that he did not agree with what they said. But both John Adams and Robert Treat Paine reported that Israel Pemberton launched into a lengthy and vituperative indictment of Massachusetts for its intolerance and insisted that that backward, narrow-minded region catch up with the rest of the enlightened colonies in regard to religious liberty. John Adams was convinced that Pemberton was "endeavoring to avail himself of this opportunity to break up the Congress."

The day after the debate the Philadelphia Baptist Association's Grievance Committee voted that the results of the conference were insufficient. They decided to give copies of Backus's tract, *An Appeal to the Public,* to all of the delegates of the Congress and to continue their efforts to press for the liberty of the Baptists.

When Backus returned to Middleborough on November 19, he encountered the rumor that the Baptists had gone to Philadelphia to drive a wedge between the New Englanders and the other colonies. As Ezra Stiles wrote in his diary, "In truth, the Baptists intend to avail themselves of this opportunity to complain to England of Persecution—because they hate Congregationalists who they know are hated by the King's Ministry & Parliament. They will leave the general Defence of American Liberty to the Congregationalists to the Northward and Episcopalians to the Southward—and make Merit themselves with the Ministry, who are glad to play them off against us, & for this End promise them Relief." It was a long time before the Baptists were able to convince their neighbors that this had not been their intent, and in 1780, when Massachusetts was writing its first state constitution, Robert Treat Paine rose in the convention to remind the delegates of the Baptists' treason in an effort to frustrate Backus's efforts to write religious liberty into the state's Bill of Rights.

The Grievance Committee of the Warren Association sent a long petition to the Massachusetts Provincial Congress which met at Cambridge in December, 1774, protesting against such slanders and against the certificate system. The petition mentioned recent persecutions in Montague, Chelmsford, Haverhill, Scarborough, Warwick, and Middleborough, and explained that the trip to the Continental Congress was an effort to seek "the future welfare of our country. . . . We remain hearty friends to our country and ready to do all in our power for its general welfare."

The Provincial Congress replied in a letter to Backus

that while it sincerely wanted to give "civil and religious liberty to each denomination in this province," it could not take such action as the Baptists wished. It is significant that the Philadelphia Grievance Committee was angry at Backus for petitioning the Provincial Congress, because this might offend the King. The Philadelphia Baptists wished Backus to have nothing to do with the revolutionary Congregationalists: It might be that ultimately "our only resource will be to apply on the other side of the Atlantic. This channel we ought ever to keep open, and not to preclude ourselves by our own conduct from being heard there with that attention and favor that our case will require."

Before Backus could call together another meeting of the Grievance Committee to consider this policy of neutralism, the battles of Lexington and Concord took place. As soon as the news reached Middleborough, Backus wrote in his diary, "those called minute-men gathered and marched off next morning." By Sunday, three days later, Backus had a sermon fit for the occasion. He preached from First Chronicles 12:32 and showed that "the doctrine of passive obedience and non-resistance to kings" brought a nation "upon the brink of popery and slavery." He "observed that if that doctrine were true George the third and his grandfather and great grandfather and the glorious king William were all usurpers and the pretender was the rightful heir of the crown." God required the people to submit to ministers "for good and . . . it was a foundation point in the constitution of the English government that the peoples property shall not be taken from them without their consent, either by themselves or their representatives." Above all, it was necessary to oppose the principle that " 'the British parliment have a right to bind America in all cases whatsoever'; which is an open violation of the essential rules of the English government." Furthermore, George III had "violated his coronation-oath which he had solemnly taken before God and his people in establishing popery in Canada [by the Quebec Act]."

The fears of the Congregationalists that the Baptists would be neutral or Tory proved false. In that moment the "we" and "they" of Baptist and Congregationalist fused into the spontaneous unity of "our" opposition to the King. Backus had no hesitancy in justifying the revolution: "Upon the whole I declared," said Backus of this sermon delivered to his anxious brethren, "I fully believed our cause was just." In the Revolution that followed, the Baptists played their part as loyally as their Congregational neighbors.

Yet the war had for them a double aspect. As Backus was to write in 1784, "While the defence of the civil rights of America appeared a matter of great importance, our religious liberties were by no means to be neglected; and the contest concerning each kept a pretty even pace throughout the war."

V I

The Massachusetts Constitution and Religious Liberty
1776–1780

"[Since] civil authority is of divine appointment, as well as ecclesiastical. . . . So there may and ought to be a sweet harmony between them." ISAAC BACKUS, *Fish Caught* (1768) p. 23

"It is readily granted that piety, religion, and morality are essentially necessary for the good order of civil society." ISAAC BACKUS, *History* (1796) p. 21

BACKUS WAS fifty-one years old when the Revolution began. His reputation had grown steadily over the years. He corresponded regularly with the leading Baptists in England, and at home he was esteemed as a denominational leader and pastor, as a writer of tracts and pamphlets, and as a trustee of the College. He had also established himself as the foremost exponent in New

England of the principles of religious liberty, to which he was to devote the next ten years.

The war itself affected him only indirectly. He preached once or twice to the troops encamped around Boston. His eldest son served in the Connecticut militia, and his brother's ironworks in Yantic supplied military and naval hardware. And he suffered, as everyone else did, from the shortages of supplies (in his case mostly paper) and the inflation of state and continental money. But no one in his family was killed or injured in the war. British troops never came close to the town of Middleborough.

Backus and the Baptists viewed the Revolution primarily as a providential act to clear the way for the overthrow of the established system. As agent for the New England Baptists in promoting this internal revolution, Backus's first step was to petition the General Assembly which convened in Watertown, Massachusetts, in September, 1775. This petition was essentially the same as that presented to the Provincial Congress a year before, but now the climate was entirely different. Several members were as ready as Backus for a major step against the establishment. Backus consulted in Watertown "with about ten of our representatives," attended the legislative sessions, and on October 5 heard his petition referred to a committee of four Congregationalists and three Baptists which "could not agree upon a bill of redress." Asaph Fletcher, a Baptist member of the legislature, therefore brought in his own bill. But the overwhelming concern with war measures prevented it from coming to a vote.

Meanwhile the Warren Association, in September, 1775, had authorized Backus to summon a Continental Congress for the Baptists to discuss the problem of religious liberty. Backus wrote "To all Christian people in the American colonies and especially to those who are of the Baptist denomination" urging them to make plans for this Congress. But the response was discouraging. William Rogers, a friend of Backus and pastor in Philadelphia, asked, "Does it not savor of an Establishment?" Others liked the idea but doubted that the time was ripe. A few favored "a plan for forming a Continental Congress of the different Denominations of Christians." A year later the Warren Association abandoned the project. Yet the proposal was a symbol of the increasing intercolonial unity among the evangelicals, and of their recognition that concerted effort was needed to keep the religious aspects of the Revolution before the public.

Massachusetts made its first effort to adopt a new constitution in 1777. That year the General Assembly had appointed a committee to prepare a draft, and early in 1778 this body organized itself as a convention to present a constitution to the voters in each town for ratification. The proposed constitution had no bill of rights, but it contained the statement that "The free exercise and enjoyment of religious profession and worship shall forever be allowed to every denomination of Protestants within this State." It said nothing about altering the existing ecclesiastical laws, for no one in New England, except the Baptists, thought that "the free exercise" of religion implied separation of Church and State.

Backus and the Grievance Committee learned of the religious conservatism of the proposed constitution late in February, 1778, and decided "it was best for us to draw up a protest against the same and try how many subscribers we can get in our whole state." Backus drew up the petition and had one hundred copies printed. It stated that no constitution should be accepted by the people of Massachusetts unless it stated as a fundamental principle "that ministers shall be supported only by Christ's authority, and not at all by assessment and secular force;

which impartial liberty has long been claimed and enjoyed by the town of Boston." How many signatures were obtained is not known, but one Baptist elder, Asa Hunt of Middleborough, reported, "I have sent you all the signers that could be procured this way; as to the people called quakers, they chuse in general that others should fight all their Battles for them; but few that I could see of them would sign altho' they acknowledged yt what we are trying for is right; strange that people should Love Liberty and not try to obtain it."

However, the Baptists had no cause to worry about the proposed constitution of 1778. There were so many objections to it by people of all persuasions that it had no chance of being ratified. Most of the towns that voted against it specifically deplored its lack of a bill of rights. Most also disliked the fact that the legislature had declared itself a constitutional convention instead of asking the people to elect delegates for that purpose. Others wanted reforms in the suffrage, the electoral districts, and the institution of a system of checks and balances, which the constitution did not provide.

Despite the defeat of this constitution the Baptists still had a major fight on their hands to end the Standing Order. In his election sermon delivered in May, 1778, the Rev. Phillips Payson of the established Congregational church in Chelsea told the assembled legislature that "The fear and reverence of God, and the terrors of eternity are the most powerful restraints upon the minds of men. . . . Established modes and usages in religion, more especially the stated public worship of God, so generally form the principles and manners of a people that changes . . . may well be esteemed very dangerous experiments in governments." Though such "innovations may be urged from the most foaming zeal," he warned, "Let the restraint of religion once be broken down, as they infallibly would be by leaving the subject of public worship to the humors of the multitude, and we might well defy all human wisdom and power to support and preserve order and government in the state."

It is significant that Payson was not only an ardent patriot in the Standing Order (he is said to have led an armed group of his own parishioners in the Battle of Lexington) but also that he was among those Arminian liberals heading toward Unitarianism. Still, he was a Puritan aristocrat in his distaste for "the multitude" and for "the foaming zeal" of pietists like the Baptists. "Persons of a gloomy, ghostly and mystic cast, absorbed in visionary scenes," he said of fanatics like Backus, "deserve but little notice in matters either of religion or government."

Backus wrote an answer which the Warren Association officially sanctioned. Published in October, 1778, under the title *Government and Liberty Described and Ecclesiastical Tyranny Exposed,* it quoted Charles Chauncy, the acknowledged leader of the Standing clergy, who had written in 1769, "We are in principle against all civil establishments in religion. It does not appear to us that God has entrusted the State with a right to make religious establishments. . . . we claim no right to desire the interposition of the State to establish that mode of worship, [church] government, or discipline we apprehend is most agreeable to the mind of Christ. We desire no other liberty than to be left unrestrained in the exercise of our principles in so far as we are good members of society." This, said Backus, in one of his most masterful strokes as a propagandist, was all that the Baptists asked. Chauncy was perfectly right in denying that one denomination had "any more right to the interposition of the civil magistrate in their favor than another."

Chauncy, of course, had argued out of fear that the Anglicans would have a favored position under an episcopate in the colonies; the Baptists complained that the Congregationalists already had such a favored position in New England. Chauncy feared that the Anglicans would tax all dissenters (as they did in England) to support their church; Backus said the Congregationalists did this now. Chauncy's arguments were, said Backus, excellent in theory: "All but Tories will allow this to be good reasoning; and why is it not as good in a Baptist as in a Presbyterian?" Backus concluded his tract with examples of more recent Baptist persecution in Massachusetts, to clinch the argument that all sects were not treated equally under the prevailing system. Payson notwithstanding, "alternatives" or "innovations" were needed.

Perhaps this tract struck home. In any case, the General Assembly tried to conciliate the Baptists by appointing a Baptist minister to deliver the election sermon the succeeding year. It was the first time any dissenter had been so honored—or was to be so honored again for a quarter century. The Baptist chosen was Backus's friend Samuel Stillman of Boston, with whom he "spent some hours . . . upon the important subject of distinguishing in his election sermon betwixt the government of Christ and yt of civil states."

Stillman was a very popular preacher; but he was also one of the more conservative Baptists, a man who John Davis considered "ruled by petticoats." His election sermon, delivered in May, 1779, was nevertheless faithful to the principle of separation. While he relied chiefly on Locke's words, he also used Backus's argument that religious taxation was taxation without representation and the Biblical argument that "the kingdom of Christ is not of this World," and therefore "the subjects of this kingdom are bound by no laws in matters of religion but such as they receive from Christ. . . . All human laws in this respect are inadmissible."

Three weeks later the General Assembly called a constitutional convention to meet in Boston in September, 1779. Backus and the Baptists girded themselves for an intensive effort to defend their principles. Backus was unquestionably the driving force in the movement. He came to Boston to lobby with the delegates; he wrote articles in the newspapers; he published new tracts; he kept abreast of every new development in the convention and informed his brethren of what was happening so that they could make their views known to their delegates. For more than two years he devoted almost all of his attention to this effort. The fact that the Baptists lost their fight only by a deceptive method of counting the ballots was a tribute to his ability. To most people the fight seemed hopeless from the outset.

Although only five of the 293 delegates to the convention are known to have been Baptists, many others were sympathetic to their ideas of religious liberty. And there was also a general disposition in the convention to allow all dissenters to state their views as fully as they wished. Since the war was still in a critical state there was every reason to avoid aggravating the opponents of the establishment. Backus could never complain that his views were not given a fair and full hearing, though he did believe that John Adams and others used unfair and misleading statements to prejudice the delegates against the Baptists.

Backus was not himself elected a delegate, but he served on the committee which drafted a list of instructions for Middleborough's representatives. The town accepted these suggestions "without alteration—one article whereof was for equal liberty of conscience and another against bribery in elections, which two articles I drew up at home and beyond my expectations they were received without any alteration by two thirds of the committee and by as large a majority of the town meetings." Similar efforts by the Baptists in other towns pressed other delegates to work for religious liberty in the convention.

Backus had another opportunity to influence the convention before it assembled. His friend, Noah Alden, a delegate from Baptist-dominated Bellingham, wrote to Backus on July 20, 1779, asking for his thoughts on a bill of rights. Backus replied in a four-page letter. The first of the thirteen basic rights he listed was, "All men are born equally free and independent, and have certain natural, inherent and unalienable rights, among which are the enjoying and defending life and liberty, acquiring, possessing, and protecting property, and persuing and obtaining happiness and safety." The second outlined his view of separation:

As God is the only worthy object of all religious worship, and nothing can be true religion but a voluntary obedience unto his revealed will, of which each rational soul has an equal right to judge for itself; every person has an unalienable right to act in all religious affairs according to the full persuasion of his own mind, where others are not injured thereby. And civil rulers are so far from having any right to empower any person or persons to judge for others in such affairs, and to enforce their judgments with the sword, that their power ought to be exerted to protect all persons and societies, within their jurisdiction, from being injured or interrupted in the free enjoyment of this right, under any pretence whatsoever.

Three years earlier George Mason, with Jefferson's approval and Madison's amendments, had written a statement on religious freedom into the Bill of Rights in the Virginia constitution:

That religion, or the duty which we owe to our Creator, and the manner of discharging it, can be directed only by reason and conviction, not by force or violence and therefore all men are equally entitled to the free exercise of religion, according to the dictates of conscience; and that it is the mutual duty of all to practice Christian forbearance, love, and charity towards each other.

Backus's tone was that of a New Light pietist; Mason's that of an Enlightened latitudinarian. The Virginians spoke of the "Creator," Backus spoke of "God." Mason stressed reason and duty, Backus stressed "religious worship." Backus referred directly to God's "revealed will" and to the "soul," Mason omitted any reference to them.

The difference was obvious and fundamental. The Virginia separationists were interested in leaving the mind free to follow its own rational direction. The Massachusetts pietists believed that separation was necessary in order to leave the "rational soul" free to find "true religion" as expressed in the Bible, "the revealed will" of God. Implicit in both statements was a belief in God, in natural law, in man's ability to find them. But the deistic separationists of Virginia trusted entirely to man's reason and free will. The pietists insisted that only through the supernatural grace of God would men find the Truth that is in Jesus Christ. Though both views were individualistic, the deist was anthropocentric, the pietist theocentric.

By a decision which was not entirely accidental, Noah Alden was chosen by the convention as chairman of the committee which was asked to draft the constitutional clauses on ecclesiastical law and practice. It turned out that the majority of the committee opposed his views, but through Alden Backus indirectly had a strong voice in that committee.

While the convention was in session, Backus was almost constantly in Boston. On November 11 a group of Baptist delegates informed him that "mr. John Adams and mr. Paine gave the convention a false acct. of the affair of my going to Philadelphia which had some influence toward procuring an article that passed yesterday which incroached upon our religious rights. It was concluded that I should answer the same in the newspaper." Backus's letter, published in the Boston *Independent Chronicle* on December 2, refuted the charges and printed the clause on religion drafted for the Bill of Rights along with criticism of it. This was the first appearance in print of that article, Article Three, and it touched off a vigorous newspaper debate on the whole problem which lasted for over a year.

Backus was stunned at the wording of Article Three: "I understand," he wrote, "that the advocates for the above article evaded all the arguments which were brought from the perfect and scriptural nature of Christ's kingdom with pretences that the article had no concern with that kingdom but only with the good of the civil state." Yet, he noted, "the article gives rulers the power of compelling people to attend and support the public worship of God; yea, and to support teachers of piety and religion; and if this is to be done without the kingdom of Christ, where are we got to?" This would create an erastian state where religion was under the complete control of the civil authorities.

The convention had not yet approved the wording of Article Three as Backus had printed it. His purpose in this and subsequent letters was to persuade the delegates to reconsider. But his efforts were in vain. The convention completed its work on March 2, 1780, and Article Three was included just as Backus had seen it in the preceding November. Backus and the Baptists now turned to the public at large. The convention had voted that the finished document should be sent to each town where it was to be considered article by article in town meeting, and a vote taken on each. The votes on each article were to be returned to the convention by June 9, at which time the convention was to re-assemble and count the returns. If any articles were not approved as drafted, the convention would then rewrite them and send them back a second time or perhaps eliminate the article entirely. The ratification process required a two-thirds majority in favor of every article before it could be adopted. Backus concentrated his efforts at persuading more than one-third of the voters to reject Article Three.

Article Three clearly altered the old ecclesiastical system. To most contemporaries it seemed a radical revision in the direction of religious equality. To Backus and the Baptists, however, it was just as unsatisfactory as the old system since it retained the principle of compulsory taxation for the support of religion. And in some respects it was worse since it seemed to make it more difficult for dissenters to obtain exemption. Backus worked for the total abrogation of Article Three and thus of the whole Puritan parish system. He approved of Article Two of the Bill of Rights: "It is the right as well as the duty of all men in society, publicly and at stated seasons to worship the SUPREME BEING, the great Creator and Preserver of the universe. And no subject shall be hurt, molested, or restrained in his person, liberty or estate, for worshipping GOD in the manner and season most agreeable to the dictates of his own conscience; or for his religious profession of sentiments; provided he doth not disturb the public peace, or obstruct others in their religious worship." That was enough.

Backus was willing to accept the first and last sentences of Article Three. These said that "the happiness of a people, and the good order and preservation of civil government, essentially depend upon piety, religion, and morality, and . . . these cannot be generally diffused through a community but by the institution of the public worship of God, and of public instruction in piety, religion, and morality. . . . And every denomination of Christians demeaning themselves peaceably, and as good subjects of the commonwealth, shall be equally under the protection of the law: and no subordination of any one sect or denomination to another shall ever be established by law."

But Backus and the Baptists vehemently opposed what came between these two sentences. Article Three also invested "their legislature with power to authorize and require . . . the several towns, parishes, precincts and other bodies politic or religious societies, to make suitable provision, at their own expense, for the institution of the public worship of GOD, and for the support and maintenance of public Protestant teachers of piety, religion, and morality. . . ." Compulsory religious taxes must be laid in each parish as they always had been.

The novel feature of Article Three, however, was that these taxes were to be laid upon all sects or for all sects. The new constitution in effect equally established all Protestant sects and put them upon the same footing in law as the Congregationalists. Any Protestant minister, of whatever sect, was guaranteed compulsory tax support and the minister of any sect could, if he received the majority of votes of a parish, become legally established. No longer did such ministers require the approbation of the neighboring Standing ministers; no longer did a majority of the members of the Standing church have to concur with the vote of the parish majority. Of course, there still might be some question as to what kind of man or set of doctrines were conformable to the definition of Protestant teaching of piety, morality, and religion; but that would now be a question for the courts to decide. It was also clearly implied that the courts would no longer use the test of a college education or knowledge of the classical languages, nor would they insist upon any sectarian doctrines. Even a Baptist or Quaker or Episcopalian could qualify as parish minister, for all were duly recognized

Protestant sects. In this respect, said the defenders of Article Three, the new system was a decided step forward for dissenters and a move toward religious equality.

The opponents of Article Three were not convinced. The new system was for them a step backward because it did away with the former system of exemption. According to Article Three, "all moneys paid by the subject to the support of public worship, and of the public teachers aforesaid, shall, if he require it, be uniformly applied to the support of the public teacher or teachers of his own religious sect or denomination, provided there be any whose instruction he attends." Everyone was required to pay religious taxes to the town treasurer who would pass them on to the ministers of each religious sect in the town in proportion to their members. To the defenders of Article Three this had the great merit of ending the question of tax dodging; it also ensured that no matter how fragmented a town or parish might become, religion would have sufficient funds to support it (something the voluntarists could not guarantee).

The question at issue was therefore the merit of a system of general assessment upon all citizens for the support of religion. The opponents of Article Three pointed out that this system indirectly gave an advantage to the Congregationalists, who constituted probably close to two-thirds of the citizens. But it is significant that the Baptists concentrated their attention on the issue of compulsory religious taxes. All of the letters, tracts, and arguments which Backus and other Baptists wrote condemning this article made three main points. They did not object to the view that Massachusetts should remain a Christian commonwealth; piety, religion, and morality could only be maintained when "the institution of the public worship of God and of public instructions in piety, religion, and morality" were "generally diffused throughout the community." The Baptists believed, however, that this general diffusion could only be effected by voluntary support, because coercion inevitably led to the infringement of individual conscience, the thwarting of true faith, and the public support of false doctrines. Finally, the Baptists were so concerned to oppose compulsory religious taxation that they ignored the more difficult question of where the line was to be drawn in regard to the public enforcement of morality, piety, and good order. Only once, for example, did Backus state his opposition to the sentence in Article Three which said that the Legislature had the "authority to enjoin upon all the subjects an attendance upon the instructions of the public teachers" of religion or upon some public worship. Many Baptists had no objection to compulsion to attend some public worship so long as the state did not prescribe the form of Protestantism. Nor did Backus and the Baptists ever protest against the fact that the Westminster Confession of Faith was inculcated into all children in the schools. Furthermore, they did not object to the prevailing Puritan laws against profanity, blasphemy, gambling, theater-going, and desecration of the Sabbath, which they accepted as within the domain of the government in its preservation of a Christian society.

Jefferson, Mason, and Madison, designing the creation of a secular state, not only opposed all such practices but also objected to the use of chaplains in the Congress and armed forces, the authorization by the state of certain days of fasting, thanksgiving, and prayer; and compulsory religious services in state universities. Jefferson explicitly stated that America was not and ought not to be a Christian country. Some of Backus's friends, after his death, were to advocate laws prohibiting the sale and manufacture of alcohol and laws preventing the delivery of the mail on Sunday as part of the Christian duty of the state. His spiritual descendants among the evangelical Baptists of the twentieth century were to argue for laws against the teaching of evolution in the public schools and for laws requiring the reading of the Bible and the recitation of prayers in the public schools. In 1791 the Warren Association joined the ministers of the Standing Order in petitioning Congress to establish a federal licensing commission to oversee the publication of all Bibles lest any errors should creep into this infallible word of God. Backus never qualified his belief in a Christian commonwealth. He consistently argued for "a sweet harmony between" Church and State. "It is readily granted," he wrote in 1784, "that piety, religion, and morality are essentially necessary for the good order of civil society." And by religion he meant Protestantism.

In the debate over Article Three which was waged between March 2 and June 9, 1780, the Baptists fought almost alone. Joseph Hawley of Northampton, a noted lawyer and leader in the Revolution, did write one letter to the convention protesting against Article Three, but it was not published. The Rev. Thomas Allen, the Standing minister of Pittsfield, a New Light Congregationalist and ardent patriot, was said to have opposed Article Three, but there is no published evidence of this; and despite his great influence Allen could not persuade his town to vote against its ratification. The only significant support the Baptists received appeared in a series of very trenchant articles signed "Philanthropos" in several Boston newspapers. The only Baptist besides Backus who entered the fray was Samuel Stillman, who wrote several letters to the newspapers under the name of "Milton," much to the disgust of several of Backus's friends who said he should have had the courage, as Backus did, to sign his own name.

The most vehement defenders of Article Three were

Samuel West, the Standing minister of Dartmouth who had been a member of the convention, and Charles Chauncy; both were liberal or Unitarian ministers. Samuel West stated the fundamental arguments in defense of a general assessment tax for religion in a series of letters to the newspapers in the months March to August, 1780 (signing them with the pen-name "Irenaeus"): "If there is no law to support religion, farewell meetinghouses, farewell ministers, and farewell religion," he wrote in the Boston *Independent Ledger* on April 17. "Good morals are necessary to promote the peace, safety and happiness of the community; religious impressions have a natural tendency to produce good morals, it being certain that the checks of conscience and the fear of divine wrath often restrain men from gross enormities." Therefore, "whatever then tends to promote religious impressions is for the civil good of society." That the churches inculcated religious doctrines as well as morality was irrelevant. The law obliged no man to believe any doctrine. Tax support of the churches was for the teaching of ethical principles based upon human observation and experience, upon logic and philosophy. To argue that the state has no right to support such teaching and no power to require everyone to attend upon it was to forget that "obedience to the whole moral law is a religious duty because it is the law of God." Undoubtedly public worship was the most effective way of enforcing moral duties. Hence it was incumbent upon the state to support public worship. All the absurd arguments of the Baptists "arise from not duly attending to nor considering that the government both of church and state is founded upon and presupposes the belief of the being and attributes of God, and of a future state of rewards and punishments."

The Bible called civil magistrates "ministers of God" because "the civil government takes in every part of religion that is necessary to make men good members of society." But by the same token, public teachers of piety and morality were civil servants, and their support by taxation was not an aspect of their spiritual duty. For the Baptists to complain that the Congregational ministers had concocted Article Three to protect their own vested interests was to misunderstand its whole point. The members of the convention were not "setting up a particular party or faction." "The teachers of every religious denomination whose principles" were "consistent with the safety of the state" could be supported. The members of the Standing Order were not crying out that "the church is in danger but that the commonwealth is in danger" from voluntarism. "The subject owes to the state whatever is important to the welfare of the state." If "attendance on the instruction of the teachers of religion or on the public worship of God is not a duty which the subjects owe to the state, it must be because religious instructions are of no advantage to the community." And who would argue that?

Implicit in West's argument was the old Puritan ideal of the corporate Christian state. Without a relationship between religious instruction and civil good, he said, "the only principle of morality" would be "self-interest." That was certainly the ultimate end of the Baptist principle, although of course they did not admit it. They clearly preferred to leave the religious welfare of society to the individual conscience and the grace of God rather than to the state. They lacked the faith of West and the incipient Unitarians in the power of reason and education, of traditions and institutions, to preserve civil order. But they had great faith in God's willingness to regenerate human nature and thereby produce voluntary obedience to his moral laws. If West's defense of a general assessment was based upon the view that most men were insufficiently committed to religion to support it voluntarily, the Baptists' opposition was based on the view that Truth was sufficiently powerful, if left unhindered by the state, to get men committed. Baptist pietism, being anti-institutional, supported a policy of laissez-faire.

Another way of stating the issues of the debate was as an argument over the nature and definition of piety—particularly whether piety was an individual or a social concern. The opponent of Article Three who signed himself "Philanthropos" in a series of newspaper letters appears to have been a New Light Congregationalist. He made four principal points, all central to the new definition of piety which had arisen out of the Awakening. Support of religion was not a civil but a spiritual duty. Nor was Christian piety or religion essential to the safety of the civil state; Greece, Rome, Pennsylvania, and New Jersey showed that "When men enter into a state of civil society, piety and religion are out of the question; they do it to promote their common interest." By piety and religion he meant specifically "gospel piety" and "heart religion," and these were not involved in the preservation of civil government. For "by far the greater part of the inhabitants of every commonwealth. . . . [are] destitute of piety or true heart religion." Finally, Philanthropos was willing to concede that morality or "natural religion" was essential to good civil government; therefore the state might employ professors to lecture on ethics and morality in each community provided they did not act as spiritual soul guides and did not conduct worship services.

Samuel West was dismayed at this definition of piety which left out the crucial aspect of "goodness of heart"; it ignored the "social and friendly sentiments towards mankind" which were the essence of benevolence and virtue and which made all men brothers. In short, it was a definition based on self-interest or selfishness, the concern of each individual for his own heart and his own salvation, which left each man an island and society a mere collection of individual souls.

It is no coincidence that Adam Smith's *Wealth of Nations,* published in 1776, provided the answer to West's question in just about the same terms that Backus and the Baptists used. The government need not direct the general welfare—by doing so it could only thwart the benevolent purpose of God; if each individual were free to follow his own self-interest, divine Providence would inevitably bring about the general welfare. For Adam Smith the divine economy of things was the natural law of supply and demand which operated as mechanically and efficiently as the Newtonian laws of gravity and motion. For the pietists of the First Great Awakening, the means by which God would regenerate men into moral beings and usher in the millennium was the law of divine grace which operated primarily through evangelism, the lively preaching of the Word pressed home to the human heart through the work of the Holy Spirit. And to the pietist the laws of grace were as knowable to man as the laws of gravity or of supply and demand. Any student of "experimental religion" could derive them from careful observation, introspection, and experience in the divine laboratory of religious revivals. Jonathan Edwards had spelled them out very clearly, so far as Backus and the Baptists of New England were concerned, in his great works on the religious affections and freedom of the will; and John Locke had provided the philosophical epistemology for them. But to Samuel West and the Unitarians in the Standing Order this was all merely "foaming zeal" and "visionary fanaticism." And while the New Light Trinitarians and Edwardseans shared the Baptist view of pietism in theory, they were too fearful of its Antinomian and perfectionist potential to abandon the establishment in favor of complete religious freedom.

In Virginia the evangelical pietists, allied with the power elite, fought successfully against the dead hand of the Anglican establishment during the Revolutionary era. In Massachusetts, where the establishment heartily embraced the Revolution and where the lay and clerical elite had the general confidence of the people, the fight took much longer. In fact, in New England Baptists sometimes bore the stigma of being Loyalists,—"disguised tories, British emissaries, profane and licentious deists, avaricious worldlings, disaffected sectaries, and furious blind bigots, who had much rather overturn the Commonwealth than not have the gratification of their own humor." Backus was specifically singled out for attack. One newspaper letter traced his ancestry to "the God of Wine" (Bacchus) and proposed a lottery to buy up all of his books—"though it is evident they are not worth the reading, still, as paper is scarce, they may be of use in a certain servile office."

When the votes of the various towns were returned and counted by the Convention on June 9, it was clear that Article Three had caused more uneasiness than any other; and it was not clear that it had the required two-thirds majority. In many towns it had received severe criticism. A majority of the voters in over sixty towns (out of 290) wished either to reject the article outright or to amend it; and in another thirty the voting was very close.

While most of the objections raised to Article Three were stated in general terms of liberty of conscience similar to those used by Locke in his *Letters on Toleration,* a few towns gave the more pietistic definition of the issue. Granville, for example, rejected Article Three by a vote of 64 to 6 because "The Article asserts that People have a Right to invest their Legislature with a Power to interfer in matters that properly belong to the Christian Church." In towns where the Baptists were numerous, such as Ashfield, Swansea, Rehoboth, Leicester, West Springfield,

Charlton, and Bellingham, Article Three was rejected outright and a substitute granting complete religious liberty
was offered in its place.

The debate over Article Three in Middleborough was
vigorous, but the Baptists were not sufficiently numerous
to carry the day. The town pointed out that the article was
"inconsistent with itself and also with other parts of the
Bill of Rights" (notably Article Two) and that "it may
Encroach upon the Consciences as well as the interests of
individuals." The town also expressed its dislike for the
fact that "individuals at Some Times and under Some
Circumstances may be Obliged . . . Contrary to the Dictates of their Consciences" for the support of religion. For
these reasons the town voted to amend the Third Article
so as to maintain the old system of tax exemption for dissenters so long as they "Let it be publickly Known" that
they were Baptists or Quakers. Presumably this meant that
they would have to submit some kind of certificate or
statement of their membership.

The returns from 220 of the 290 towns reveal a vote of
8,885 persons for accepting Article Three as written and
6,225 for rejecting or amending it in some way. Only two
counties had a majority against the article: Suffolk (in
which Boston was located) and Bristol (which had always
been the center of Baptists and Quakers in the state). The
Bostonians opposed it because they feared that it might
abrogate their traditional freedom from religious taxes.

According to the strict rules of the convention, Article
Three did not obtain the required two-thirds majority;
it obtained only 59 percent. The article therefore should
have been revised by the convention and re-submitted to
the towns in a new form designed to meet their objections.
But the tellers counted as being in favor of the article all
returns which were not outright rejections; and it must be
said that many of the returns were so confusingly stated

in regard to what should be done about the article that it would have been extremely difficult for the convention to arrive at any formulation which would have obtained more votes in its favor. Hence the convention declared that Article Three, like every other article, had received the requisite majority and therefore approved the new constitution. It was now up to the legislature to give its formal concurrence at its October session.

Some Baptists wished Backus to continue his protests by petitioning the legislature to rescind Article Three, although others feared it would "answer no valuable purpose." Backus, of course, wished to fight on until compulsory taxes were abolished, for he knew of the juggling of the returns through Noah Alden, who gave him a precise report of the votes. The Warren Association, on September 12, 1780, agreed to protest and raised money to circulate a petition against Article Three.

This petition, which repeated the Baptist arguments, was ignored by the legislature, and the new constitution was ratified. Early in the spring of 1781, Backus's tract entitled *Truth Is Great and Will Prevail* voiced the general disappointment of the Baptists at the failure of their efforts and expressed their determination to continue the fight. In September of that year the Warren Association again delegated Backus to protest against the continued persecution of Baptists who refused, from conscience, to pay religious taxes. On October 5, 1781, Backus's circular letter on behalf of the Grievance Committee urged the Baptists to continue passive resistance: "brethren, face them down boldly upon this point [freedom of conscience] and they cannot stand." Whatever expenses might occur through the refusal to pay would "be made equal by collecting money for said purpose among the churches."

However, the Baptists could expect no help from the

legislature. The new system of general assessment for religion was imbedded in the constitution. The only hope now lay through the courts, which might see the same contradiction within the constitution that so many towns had pointed out. How could the bill of rights both grant full religious liberty to all citizens and yet tax some against conscience? The courts could declare that liberty of conscience must take precedence and thereby invalidate that part of Article Three which required all to pay religious taxes.

Backus and the Grievance Committee may have been persuaded to resort to the courts by the case of the Negro slave, Quok Walker, who in 1781 sued his master on the grounds that the state constitution declared all men born free and equal. The court ruled that this inalienable natural right, imbedded in the first article of the bill of rights, took precedence over the laws of slavery and of property. A similar decision might grant religious liberty to dissenters.

Elijah Balkcom of Attleborough brought the case which tested the constitutionality of Article Three. Balkcom, a regular attendant (though not a baptized member) of the Baptist Church in the east parish of North Attleborough not far from where Backus lived, refused to pay the religious tax. None of the Baptists in his church did so or turned in certificates. Five members, each taxed about six dollars, saw the constable sell one of their cows at auction. But Balkcom was arrested and carried off toward Taunton jail. He paid his tax under duress, together with a fee of one shilling for the constable's costs, and then brought suit against the assessors for taxing him illegally and contrary to his constitutional right of freedom of conscience.

William Holmes, Esq., justice of the peace in Norton, Massachusetts, who tried the case on February 22, 1782,

declared that Balkcom had been properly taxed. Balkcom
then appealed to the county court which met in Taunton
on March 12, 1782. Backus went over to attend and to act
as a witness for Balkcom. Balkcom was represented by
the Hon. William Bradford, Esq. and James Mitchell Varnum, Esq., both prominent lawyers. The parish had obtained the best lawyer it could find to defend its assessors
—Robert Treat Paine, the Attorney General of the State.
After a "learned and elegant" argument, said Backus,
"lawyer Paine moved to have Elijah Balkcom's case taken
out of court and refer'd to particular men"—i.e., to a
board of arbitration. Backus and Balkcom decided not to
consent because their "aim was to know how the judges
understood the present laws in these matters." Only a legal decision from the bench would give the Baptists the
precedent they wanted.

The case hinged on the means by which a Baptist, or
any other dissenter, was to obtain the religious liberty
which the constitution guaranteed to all citizens. The assessors had said that they would not have taxed Balkcom
had he turned in a certificate. Bradford and Varnum argued that the certificate laws were no longer in effect since
the constitution had made any such system invalid by the
guarantee that no sect should ever be subordinate to another. If the Baptists had to give certificates to the parish
to obtain religious freedom, that in fact made them subordinate to Congregationalists. Lawyer Paine "pleaded
that giving certificates was not a subordination to any sect,
but to the government." "After the judges had deliberated
upon it," Backus noted, "they unanimously gave judgment
that the appelant recover damages & costs." The Baptists
had won a great victory. This "very important event,"
wrote Backus, meant "deliverance" from oppression at
last. For the court, by its decision, had virtually said no
dissenters need ever again submit certificates and no par-

ish assessors could ever again tax, distrain, or imprison them for not so doing. The establishment was overthrown.

At its annual meeting a few months later, the Warren Association linked the Balkcom decision with the Treaty of Paris which ended the Revolution that same year; both were proofs of God's blessing upon America. The association's letter to the churches made explicit the relationship between the fight against political tyranny in Britain and religious oppression in Massachusetts: The Revolution, which assured all men equal rights and founded all righteous government on compact had extended to religious affairs. "God has taken the wise in their own craftiness" for "the last clause" of Article Three "overthrows the superstructure which was intended to have been built thereon."

Backus's pamphlet the same year, *A Door Opened for Equal Christian Liberty and No Man Can Shut It,* explained the details of the case. He was content, even though the Congregationalists could still lay taxes on themselves and use the power of the state to collect them. Baptists were free of any obligation which acknowledged the power of the state over them.

The Baptists' rejoicing was premature. The decision of one county court did not bind the other courts. Two years later another case reversed the Balkcom decision and cast Backus into a slough of despond from which he never fully emerged.

The case of Cutter *v.* Frost involved the Baptists in the West or second parish of Cambridge. In 1784 three members of this church, one of whom was Gershom Cutter, were distrained for refusing to pay their religious taxes. Cutter brought suit against the assessors and the county court in Concord in September, 1784, followed the Balkcom precedent and awarded damages to Cutter for trespass. But the parish appealed to the Superior Court. On

October 26, 1784, "Judge Sergeant," speaking for this court, "declared their old laws [regarding certificates] to be in force and that they [the court] knew no society in the Commonwealth but corporate bodies; with whom Judge Sewall concurred, and the jury turned the case against the Baptists the next day. The other judges said little upon the case."

Elder Thomas Green, pastor of the Baptist Church in West Cambridge, expressed the consternation this decision caused among the Baptists: "We have lost our case. The Judges gave a most shocking arbitrary Exposition upon ye Third Article of ye Bill of Rights. They declare no Society that is not under corporate Power is known in the Law in this Commonwealth[;] also that ye Temporary Acts for the Quakers and Baptists and Churchmen are still in full force and that the Third Article is perfectly conformable to said Laws—also that Jewrors were obliged to determine our cause upon such Principals." As a result "The Parish Treasurer has given orders to these Collectors amediately to strain upon [distrain] the rest of my hearers for Taxis which will amount to *100* dollars."

Green's report was somewhat in error. Had the old exemption laws still been in effect, the Baptists would have been entitled to exemption if they gave in certificates. But Article Three had specifically stated that no one was exempt. The court appears rather to have said that in order to have their taxes paid over to their own church, the dissenters had to file a certificate so that the treasurer would know to whom to turn over the money.

The decision made another and far more devastating point about the rights of dissenters under Article Three. It stated that only religious societies incorporated by law were under any circumstances entitled to legal recognition. Therefore most, if not all, Baptist churches in existence in Massachusetts in 1784 were illegal or extra-legal, voluntary, private associations. To be incorporated, each dissenting congregation would have to petition the legislature to obtain a charter. On the other hand, all Standing parishes were automatically incorporated by law at the time their boundaries were laid out. The decision in effect held that no one was exempt from paying taxes to support the Standing church in each parish.

The reasoning by which the court arrived at this decision was tortuous, and was to be vigorously debated for twenty years before Chief Justice Theophilus Parsons finally rendered a definitive statement on it in 1810. The decision in the Cutter case maintained that the phrase "religious societies" in Article Three simply modified the term "bodies politic" and that it did not signify a voluntary religious association as opposed to an incorporated one. The convention delegates do not appear to have put this interpretation on their phrase, nor did any of those who argued about the matter in the newspapers or in the town meetings. It had not been considered necessary for dissenting churches, congregations, or religious societies to incorporate in order to be exempt from religious taxes before 1780. And if anyone had construed Article Three as Judge Sergeant did, surely some dissenting sect would have protested or at least have applied to the legislature for incorporation as soon as the constitution went into effect.

Hence the consternation with which the Baptists greeted the Cutter decision. It reversed the Balkcom decision and thereby closed the door to liberty which Backus had so confidently said could not be shut. It also denied any way for the Baptists to avoid supporting the parish churches except by petitioning the legislature for incorporation. And such a petition was an even more flagrant infringement of conscience than giving in certificates; it acknowledged the power of the State over the Church—

the power to incorporate some and not others according to its own standards.

Four days after the Cutter decision was announced, Backus called a meeting of the Grievance Committee in Boston. He had taken the trouble to consult "a great lawyer" (perhaps James Sullivan) about the crisis they faced. This lawyer had pointed out a way to escape the dilemma of petitioning for incorporation. He had suggested that the Baptists file certificates, pay their taxes, and then, if the parish treasurer refused to turn their tax money over to their own pastor, bring suit. But this advice rested upon a reading of Article Three even more strained than that of the judges in the Cutter Case. Moreover, it would put the Baptist elders in the unenviable position of suing parish treasurers in court, perhaps yearly, for each of their members' taxes—a situation which would have the effect upon the public mind of making these elders seem litigious and avaricious.

The Grievance Committee voted four to one to follow the lawyer's advice. Backus cast the negative vote. He did so on two grounds: it put the elders in an embarrassing position and, more important, it was a reversal of the stand of 1773 against giving in certificates and a surrender to expediency. He was over-ruled by three of the "learned" ministers from the Middle Colonies, and by one younger man. Samuel Stillman's conservative vote was to be expected. That of Hezekiah Smith, a Princeton graduate and the well-to-do pastor of one of the wealthiest churches in the state, was also not surprising. Isaac Skillman, Princeton '66, had succeeded John Davis as pastor of the Second Baptist Church of Boston, and in 1790 returned to New Jersey for the rest of his life; he was never active in the fight for disestablishment. Caleb Blood was pastor of the well-to-do Baptist church in Newton, Massachusetts. Not a member of the learned ministry, Blood was born in Worcester, Massachusetts in 1754. Three years after casting his vote in this turning point in Baptist policy, he moved to Vermont, where he remained for the next twenty years. Backus was the only one of the five members of the committee who was a Separate-Baptist and who had lived through the critical years of the Great Awakening in New England. He was the most pietistic among them. The others took a more pragmatic and urbane view of the problem; the spirit of the times did not call for martyrdom and fanaticism. They were more interested in improving the status and respectability of their denomination than in tilting against windmills.

The committee therefore advised Elder Thomas Green to make the first test case for this new approach to the problem. Green "sued for the money in three cases before three different justices of the peace." And as the great lawyer had predicted, he "recovered judgment"; the justices interpreted Article Three to mean that the parish treasurers must turn over the tax money of Green's members or regular worshipers to him. "Then their enemies appealed to concord court where after a full hearing on March 18, 1786, the cases were turned in the baptists favor; upon which the parish made up with them." The Baptists had thus found a way out of their dilemma, though not a very tidy one.

It left their legal status more confused than ever, for it seemed to negate the ruling that only members of incorporated religious societies were recognized in the law. Would other county courts, would the Superior Court, be bound by the decisions in Green's cases? It would have proved a hollow victory if Baptists were once again compelled to return to the certificate system and endure long and costly trials in order to sue the money which was rightfully theirs out of the hands of malicious parish treasurers. In the following years many Baptist elders were forced to do as Green had done, and it was reported that "it required in one instance fourteen suits at law before a town treasurer yielded the taxes, and in another an expense of one hundred dollars and four year's time to get four dollars out of his hands for the use of a Baptist minister." In many cases the Baptists lacked the funds to prosecute such cases and had to let their tax money go to the support of the parish church.

On the other hand, it also happened in many towns and parishes, that once the Baptists proved they had the determination and funds to bring a suit, the Standing Order ceased to argue the matter. There the system returned to the *status quo ante:* the Baptists turned in certificates, as they had prior to 1780, and the parish assessors simply omitted their names from the religious tax lists.

For Backus the outcome of his twelve-year battle against compulsory religious taxes was a bitter disappointment. In 1773 his hopes had been high. The fervor for natural rights growing out of the disputes with the mother country seemed to foretell new victories. In the end, however, the momentum for revolution against the traditions of the past had stopped short of the goal. The new constitution had, it was true, instituted some revolutionary changes in the Church-State system, but not such as satisfied Backus. Somehow the Puritans (now the Yankees) had proven sufficiently resilient to contain the fervor which had raged since 1740 with only a minimum of institutional change. It took Jefferson's "Second Revolution" in 1800 and the Second Great Awakening finally to shake down the old walls of custom.

But if its institutions were intact, the mood of New England was very different. The great majority of the people no longer viewed the established church in the same light. Nor did they fear the "Munsterite" tendencies of the Baptists as formerly. The Baptists had been loyal patriots and most towns took an increasingly lenient attitude toward them. Sporadic cases of persecution continued, and there were even instances of mob action against Baptist itinerants during these years. But by 1785 a climate of broad toleration was pervasive. An increasing number of towns and parishes voted the Baptists a general and permanent exemption. Fewer and fewer cases of oppression were reported to the Grievance Committee after 1785. Backus regretted the decline in pietistic fervor for this cause among his brethren, but he had to admit that there was less occasion for militant action.

He therefore turned his zeal to other outlets. As the threat to the Baptists' liberty declined, the threat to their doctrines increased. The breakdown of the Calvinistic consensus which had dominated the colonial mind for 150 years, the influence of the Enlightenment, and the sectarian innovations engendered by the Great Awakening produced a host of new sects and ideologies which found fertile ground among the Baptists. To Backus all were threats to Truth. And even while he was fighting the political battle for religious liberty, he had to devote an increasing amount of his time after 1770 to combating these spiritual delusions.

VII
Defender of the
Baptist Faith
1770–1790

*"The Methodists have followed the Baptists thro'
the country with much zeal, but they earnestly
strike against the most essential doctrines of the
gospel. . . . To hold up light against their errors,
and others, is of great importance in this time when
many have an ear to hear."* ISAAC BACKUS, ms.
letter to his wife from Virginia, May 9, 1789.

IN A SENSE Backus was right to consider his battles to maintain the purity of the New Light doctrines
of grace and to advance the truths of antipedobaptism
more important than his efforts to separate Church and
State. The Baptist movement as the vanguard of evangelicalism, in the long run, had the more far-reaching consequences for the development of the American temper. His
work as a polemical defender of the faith fell into two
distinct phases. At first he was champion of the Separate-
Baptist movement against perfectionists, pedobaptists or
anti-revivalists within the ranks, and against the attacks
of the Standing Order from outside. But after 1770 he was

compelled to combat the gradual erosion of strict Calvinist doctrine and the continual inroads of radical new sects
among the Separate-Baptists. As the fragmentation of the
old Calvinist consensus continued at an increasing pace
throughout America at the end of the eighteenth century,
Backus devoted more and more of his writing and evangelism to combating new heresies and erroneous practices.
The Baptist movement, by virtue of its highly volatile
pietism, its extremely loose polity, and its unsophisticated
ministers and laity, was more susceptible to new religious movements than any other in New England.

The Age of Reason produced an ever-increasing
number of persons who doubted the predestinarian assumptions of Calvinism. Backus himself shared some of
the more optimistic views of his day concerning the in-
evitability of progress (particularly the progress of the
Baptists and of the United States) and concerning the
benevolence of God (who had so obviously chosen America for the scene of his new reformation in religious and
political liberty). But Backus framed his optimism in pietistic millennial terms and had no difficulty in assimilat-
ing it into his Calvinistic faith. There was no contradiction
between predestination and the rising glory of America,
nor between a vigorous activism to promote God's will
and the doctrine of election (or man's inability to effect
his own salvation). Since men were morally responsible
agents, they were obligated to "strive to enter in at the
gate." God had called the saints of the new reformation,
the Baptists in particular, to lead mankind to the millennium in America.

To many intellectuals the creed of deism seemed more
in harmony with the enlightened age in which they lived;
Jefferson and Thomas Paine had nothing but scorn for
Calvinism and the other "outworn" creeds and "supersti-
tions" of the Age of Faith. Other intellectuals, especially

in New England, had a less anticlerical reaction to the Enlightenment and, like John Adams and Robert Treat Paine, became Unitarians. But few Baptists were intellectuals, and while Backus more than once displayed his scorn for "infidelity" in both its deistic and Unitarian forms, he never felt that the new reformation was sufficiently threatened by either to devote a whole tract to them.

Yet Backus recognized that the Age of Revolution had produced a new and exhilarating climate of change, of exuberant experimentation, and of self-confident freedom which worked both for and against the Separate-Baptist movement. The three major forces which molded the mood and actions of Americans in the last quarter of the eighteenth century were the new experimental or pietistic religion of the Awakening, the new science and philosophy of the Enlightenment, and the new politics of the Revolution. The Separate-Baptists were peculiarly susceptible to all three. Having found a new basis for religious knowledge and practice, they experimented with any new form of religious expression or organization which seemed to them to offer Truth. Once the Puritan system was rejected, a whole host of new possibilities for achieving direct, personal, renewable, experiential relationships with God arose. Backus wanted to confine this ebullient pietism of the age within the bounds of Calvinistic theology, Separate-Baptist polity, and revivalistic worship. But having opened Pandora's box, the Separate-Baptists were powerless to shut it. Until 1780 their movement remained united against the restraints of the establishment. With the new freedom after the Revolution and the recognition that the establishment had become a dead letter, this pietistic movement scattered in all directions.

The political revolution which succeeded the religious revolution of the Awakening amplified the latent individualism of Americans inordinately, and the frontier became both the symbol and the laboratory for their new freedom. The breakdown of royal authority meant the breakdown of the old corporate ideal. After 1770 government rested in the hands of the towns, and with the rapid settlement of new areas in western and northern New England, as well as in hitherto unsettled pockets eastward, the Separate-Baptists found new means to exercise their freedom and pursuit of Truth. They ceased to think and act like a persecuted, hole-in-the-corner sect and entered into the mainstream of American life—particularly in Maine, New Hampshire, Vermont, and western Massachusetts. Many sought freedom from their own denominational leaders as well as from the Puritan and Royal authorities. What many adventurous and individualistic Separate-Baptists saw as new opportunities for freedom, however, Backus often saw as threats to divine Truth and gospel order.

He devoted most of his thirty-seven tracts and his sermons to four major threats—the Shaker movement, the Universalists, the Methodists, and the Freewill Baptists. Lesser dangers emanated from the Old or Six-Principle Arminian Baptists, the Sandemanians, and the hyper-Calvinistic neo-Edwardseans or Hopkinsians. While Backus agreed with Jefferson that in the long run the Truth would win out in any free competition for the minds and hearts of men, he also believed that in the short run Satan was a serious adversary, and it was therefore the duty of those strong in the Truth to contend for it by every means at their command. The Christian life was an endless battle with Satan for the souls of men. Since Backus fought vigorously to undermine the old regulatory practices of Puritanism by which the state enforced conformity, he felt doubly anxious to prove that the Truth could maintain itself in the free marketplace of ideas.

Backus's first tract in defense of Calvinism, *True Faith*

Will Produce Good Works (1767) was prefaced by an attack upon the errors of the opposite extreme, hyper-Calvinism, as it was currently being preached by Robert Sandeman. Sandeman was a Scotsman who had broken away from the established Presbyterian Church and joined the followers of John Glas in Perth before emigrating to New England in 1764. He founded churches in Portsmouth, New Hampshire and in Boston. Backus pointed out that Sandeman falsely attacked "The distinction between *doctrinal* and *experimental* knowledge; between right *notions* of the truth in the *head* and *knowing* them in the *heart*." Like so many hyper-Calvinistic "legalists" he had over-emphasized an intellectual comprehension of the intricacies of doctrine and underemphasized the ability of the ordinary person to experience religion in his heart, and thus to know for certain that he was saved. When Sandeman argued that "No mortal can attain any such assurance of hope but that he still finds himself occasionally in regard of losing it," Backus bridled at the thought that a true convert might ever doubt the inward change wrought in his soul by the Holy Ghost. Backus also deplored Sandeman's excessive preaching of hellfire and damnation: "A preacher, says he [Sandeman], runs no risk of exceeding in urging the motives of fear"; but Sandeman failed to distinguish between a "slavish" fear (a mere "fear of death") and "the reverence and godly fear [awe] whereby gracious persons serve God." Sandeman believed that Whitefield and even Edwards had offered too much encouragement to the sinner by claiming that he could make some effort toward his own salvation. And finally Sandeman was guilty of introducing many erroneous practices into his worship such as "the kiss of charity" whereby "at the admission of members and at other opportunities they salute each other with a kiss of charity"; he advocated a return to the primitive practice of footwashing among the saints; and he insisted that all church decisions be taken unanimously rather than by majority rule.

Sandeman's doctrines according to Backus had the natural result of turning people against any form of Calvinism. People recoiled in horror, saying that the doctrine of election made God "a respecter of persons" and that by predestination "we make men mere machines who are not worthy of praise or blame."

The bulk of the tract attacked those who, having rejected Calvinism entirely, adopted the Arminian notions of the freedom of the will and "the modern scheme" that "they will receive nothing for truth but what they can comprehend with their reason." To these misguided souls Backus answered, "Nothing is more certain than this, that a God which a creature can comprehend is an idol." Jonathan Edwards, Backus noted, had effectively answered the Arminians in his magnificent discourse on *The Freedom of the Will.* Edwards had clearly proved that it was because men would not obey God, not because they could not, that they were damned. There was nothing unreasonable in God's punishing men for persistence in doing wrong despite their clear knowledge of truth as revealed in Scripture. God, out of his sovereign grace and mercy, chose to save a few persons whom he elected arbitrarily; and none had the right to complain "against God's doing what he will with his own grace."

The Sandemanians did not reply to Backus's tract, but some of the General or Six-Principle Baptists in the area of Rhode Island and southeastern Massachusetts did. Elder Daniel Martin, pastor of the Old Baptist Church in Rehoboth, wrote a tract entitled *Some Meditations on the Plaine Testimony of the Holy Scriptures Relating to the Elect* (1770) which defended Arminianism against Backus's slurs. Backus then rebutted Martin in a tract entitled *The Doctrine of Sovereign Grace Opened and Vindicated* (1771), sub-titled, *The Consistency and Duty of declaring Divine Sovereignty and Man's Impotency, while yet we address their Consciences with the Warnings of Truth and Calls of the Gospel.* He was particularly shocked by Martin's assertion that "Since it is the good will of God that all men should be saved and come to the knowledge of the truth, what doth hinder, or indeed what can hinder or prevent [men's obtaining salvation] but the want of man's good will?" Martin believed, as did most Arminians, in the theory of the General Atonement or General Redemption—that Christ had died so that *all* men might be saved who believed in him and not just so that a few elect might be chosen at random by God. But, said Backus, this made God's plan of salvation dependent upon man's free will. If all men could be saved and each could choose whether to save himself or not, then God was dependent upon man who could frustrate His design for salvation. Martin's "plan would make the will of the Creator dependent on the will of the creature." Contrary to the laws of philosophy and psychology as expounded by Edwards, Arminians argued that men can "act with or against motive."

The dispute with Daniel Martin was part of Backus's long-term controversy with the Old Baptists, most of whom had been won over to the Calvinistic views of the Separate-Baptists by the Revolution. Martin's own church collapsed after his death in 1781. Ironically at that very time the Freewill Baptist movement began in New Hampshire and swept away a large part of the Separate-Baptist gains on the northern frontier. Eventually the Freewill Baptists moved southward, invading Backus's own region and reviving the waning Arminianism in southeastern Massachusetts. Backus reported in his diary in 1799 that a revival among the Baptists in Marshfield "went on gloriously until one Benjamin Randel, an arminian baptist of Newhampshire, came there in March and laboured for above a fortnight" until he produced a schism in the Marshfield church and wrecked the revival.

Benjamin Randall, generally reputed to be the founder and moving force behind the Freewill Baptist movement, had been converted under the preaching of George Whitefield in 1770. Whitefield, of course, was an orthodox Calvinist and much admired by Backus, but his preaching seemed clearly to imply that salvation was within the grasp of all his hearers and that they might expect conversion under his preaching if they would only repent and turn from their sins. Randall followed the usual New Light pattern, first joining the Standing Church after his conversion, then separating from it because it was too corrupt, then becoming an antipedobaptist, and finally feeling the call to preach. He organized a church in New Durham, New Hampshire, and became its pastor, but in 1779 several Baptist ministers in the vicinity refused to have fellowship with him because they said he was an Arminian. He told his congregation that he would not preach the faith of Calvinism "Because I did not believe in it." Several other Separate-Baptist ministers in the area agreed with him and in 1780 Randall, Edward Lock, and Tozier Lord formed the new Freewill denomination. For the next thirty years they fought a vigorous battle with the Calvinists in New Hampshire, Maine, Vermont, and finally in Massachusetts. By 1810 there were one hundred churches in the new denomination in New England.

Randall's Arminianism did not make faster headway in Massachusetts because the Universalists anticipated them. While Randall was still forming his first churches in New Hampshire in the 1780's, the Universalist movement swept through Massachusetts and picked up a host of former Separate-Baptists no longer satisfied with Calvinism. Universalism was not simply a lower class form of Unitarianism. Many respectable and educated persons adopted universalist views, like Charles Chauncy of Boston (though he did not feel called upon to leave his Congregational pulpit for this reason). Moreover, early Universalism was extremely pietistic in the rural areas and not at all imbued with the rationalism of urban Unitarians. Above all, Universalism drew its converts less from among the Standing churches than from the Separate-Baptists. It did share with Unitarianism, as with the Freewill Baptists, the general antipathy toward the more rigid aspects of orthodox Calvinism. And it shared with the Separate-Baptists an intense hostility toward the established ecclesiastical system. In fact, after Backus's death, when his denomination had achieved respectability and status, and its leaders became preoccupied with competing for converts in the home and foreign missionary zeal of the day, the Universalists came forward as the most vigorous advocates of separation of Church and State in Massachusetts.

The origins of the Universalist denomination lay in the work of an English minister named John Murray, who came to America in 1770 and founded the first Universalist church in Gloucester, Massachusetts, in 1779. Backus first mentioned the doctrine of universalism in his diary on October 25, 1778, when he reported, "John Murray has again been here of late preaching up universal salvation with much art and eloquence and had many followers, but as to true religion, people are exceedingly stupid about it." A year later he reported that Gamaliel Reynolds, the elder of the Separate Church in Norwich, and John Tyler, the Episcopal minister in Norwich, had both fallen in with Murray "and multitudes flock after him." By 1781 so many Baptist churches had begun to lose members to "the universalist delusion" or "the universalers" that

Backus felt he had better take action. His tract, *The Doctrines of Universal Salvation Examined and Refuted* (1782) not only attacked John Murray, but also Charles Chauncy, James Relly (the English Universalist), and Elhanan Winchester, a Separate-Baptist of great repute who had announced his conversion to Universalism in the First Baptist Church of Philadelphia.

Each of these men arrived at the doctrine of universal salvation by his own road; and others later, like Hosea Ballou and Caleb Rich, followed yet different paths. When Murray arrived in America in 1770 he did not dare to proclaim himself a Universalist until he had first obtained a large following among New Lights who were unable to distinguish between his preaching and that of Whitefield (by whom Murray had been converted). At first Murray simply avoided the subjects of hellfire, damnation and reprobation, then he confessed that he did not believe in them. God was too benevolent to make men suffer damnation through all eternity, and he believed that Christ had died so that all men might ultimately be saved. He and later Universalists quarreled over whether those who died without conversion would suffer some temporary torments as punishment or would rise at once to heaven.

Elhanan Winchester (like Hosea Ballou and Caleb Rich) started as a Separate-Baptist. He became pastor of an open-communion Separate church in Rehoboth in 1771. Within a year he adopted closed-communion views which split his church, and he was dismissed. He then had great success as an itinerant evangelist all up and down the East Coast from 1771 to 1780. Backus considered him one of the most gifted preachers in the denomination and recommended him highly to his "western brethren" in 1780 when they were looking for a pastor for the First Baptist Church of Philadelphia. When Winchester defected to Universalism a year after attaining this prestigious post, and when he carried most of that church with him, Backus and the New England Baptists were astounded and abashed.

Charles Chauncy, on the other hand, had simply carried his well-known Unitarian tendencies and his belief in the benevolence of the Deity to their logical conclusion when he adopted universalism. He had started writing his *Salvation for All Men* in the 1760's but did not dare publish it till 1781. Chauncy's defection to universalism caused almost as much consternation in the Standing churches as Winchester's among the Separate-Baptists. But Chauncy had no use for Murray, Winchester, and the "illiterate" preachers of universalism and made no effort to join them.

Backus was not surprised to find this heresy creeping into the Standing churches, but he was deeply shocked to find it among so many of the foremost members of the new reformation. He recognized the variations among these enemies of Calvinism, but all the Universalists rejected the doctrines of arbitrary grace, reprobation, and eternal hellfire. In place of a sovereign and righteous God of Justice, "Relly," said Backus, "builds upon an imaginary union with Jesus, but Winchester upon the benevolent nature of the Deity." "Relly holds that salvation is already compleat in Christ" so as to exempt men from all future punishment; but Winchester treats sin "as a natural and not a moral evil; as a calamity rather than a crime." Relly, however, "declares sin to be an infinite evil, deserving of infinite punishment," but he insists that this punishment has been paid by Christ in the atonement. Chauncy, like Relly, emphasizes the benevolence of the Deity, who would not confine any soul to everlasting torment.

For Backus the whole system was "a filthy dream," an insult to God, a delusion of the Devil, a mockery of revelation, and a refutation of all human experience. Backus in this tract revealed how close he was to the defenders of

the establishment in his belief in the necessity of incul-
cating religion as an essential basis for maintaining the
stability, morality, and order of a Christian commonwealth: "No government can be maintained in civil states
without appeals to God to avenge injustice, perjury, and
unfaithfulness." He probably agreed with Robert Treat
Paine that there was some doubt whether Universalists
could claim tax exemption as Protestant teachers of piety,
religion, and morality under Article Three. Not until 1786
were Murray and his lawyer, James Sullivan, able to convince a jury (over the opposition of the Unitarian judges)
that a Universalist who denied eternal damnation was
nevertheless entitled to be called a Protestant teacher of
piety, religion, and morality.

Backus's later restatement of his own belief in eternal
hellfire and his opposition to Universalism rested on the
Lockean argument of private property. God was the owner
in fee simple of the universe and its inhabitants, including
the devils in hell. He could show mercy to whom he would.
"To deny this is to deny him the right which every free-
man has with his own property." The tract of 1782, however, did little to halt the movement away from Calvinism.
Other Separate-Baptist ministers soon turned Universalist,
and almost every Baptist church in New England reported
some defections to this "delusion."

Like Unitarianism, the Universalist denomination
never became large. Its doctrines, though in general harmony with the optimistic and benevolent spirit of the age,
were too much at variance with traditional Christian orthodoxy. Backus eventually came to believe that it did
more harm to the Standing churches than to the Separate-
Baptists. In 1796 he wrote to a friend concerning a new
defense of Universalism by Dr. Joseph Huntington, a
follower of Chauncy: "How popular has this doctrine

grown? Though it strikes at the root of all true religion, as much as infidelity [deism] itself. But it has had an influence towards pulling down what men have called their established religion in New England. Dr. Huntington had been a great leader therein. Thus God makes all things work for the good of his children."

Fortunately for the Baptists in New England their most serious rival, the Methodist church, did not reach that region until the 1790's, by which time the Baptists were firmly entrenched. Moreover, the growth of Methodism was hindered in New England by its old association with Toryism—Wesley having opposed the Revolution and having instructed his followers to do the same—by its episcopal form of church government, and by a clear doctrine of perfectionism which, combined with its fervent exhorting by illiterate preachers, made the New Englanders cautious. On the other hand, its Arminian tendencies, its doctrine of general redemption, and its dedication to experimental heart religion appealed to pietists dissatisfied with Calvinism. Moreover, it did not tamper with the familiar doctrines of infant baptism, hellfire, and damnation.

Backus first called attention to the dangers and errors of Methodism in 1784. The second volume of his history of the Baptists described "a new sect which is now formed in America" which was Arminian in theology and episcopal in polity. "They allow no man to be a preacher in their church but such as profess a belief that perfection is attainable in this life." John Wesley, said Backus, "held that Christ died equally for all mankind, but that men are saved by their own faith and obedience, which yet they may fall from and perish forever." Backus particularly deplored Wesley's statements that "all true believers are in Scripture termed the elect," and that "He that believeth shall be saved; he that believeth not shall be damned,"—views which many Americans found very attractive.

Backus drew on Biblical texts taken from the Westminster Confession of Faith to uphold all the five points of Calvinism and to prove that Wesley distorted Scripture. The Methodists had "taken great pains to draw off people from all other religious communities in our land by confounding works and grace together." They, like the Universalists, exalted man at the expense of God's sovereignty. Though Backus still found it necessary to "hold up light against their errors" in 1790, the Methodists made very slow progress in Massachusetts during his lifetime—perhaps because the Freewill Baptists and Universalists had already garnered most of the lower class anti-Calvinists.

The Baptists who were attracted to the Shaker movement after 1770 revealed an additional facet of the new reformation. The pietism of the Awakening contained the same tendency toward Antinomian mysticism which had been implicit in Puritanism from the outset. Backus thought he had successfully repressed this tendency in the movement in the 1750's when it erupted in the immortalist errors of Shadrach Ireland, Ebenezer Ward, and John Phinney. But in the 1780's it carried some eminent leaders into the new denomination founded by "Mother" Ann Lee.

Shakerism, or the United Society of Believers, came to America from Manchester, England, in 1774, in the person of Ann Lee. She had separated from her husband and joined the Shaking Quakers in 1758. Their worship differed from the quiet meetings of the other Friends by stressing the importance of dancing, singing, and prophesying in tongues. Ann Lee proved to be a very eloquent and forceful exponent of these pentecostal or Antinomian practices, though she herself was virtually uneducated.

In America she and eleven followers formed a small community in Watervliet, New York, nine miles northeast of Albany. They farmed on a communal basis and practiced celibacy as well as their peculiar form of dancing and singing worship. They were distrusted by the local authorities. Suspected of Toryism because they were newly arrived from Britain and were pacifists, they faced increasing hostility from their neighbors during the Revolution.

"Mother" Ann made an evangelistic tour through western New England to search for a more friendly site for her community. Traveling through Pittsfield, Ashfield, Cheshire, and Harvard, Massachusetts between 1781 and 1783, the Shakers made many converts, most of them from among the Separate-Baptists. They finally settled in Harvard, buying the house which Shadrach Ireland had built for his Immortalist group and in which he died in 1780.

The theology and practices of the Shakers appealed to the more radical pietists who had found a temporary home among the Baptists after the Awakening. A direct personal communion with the Holy Spirit pervaded the Shaker meetings and their daily lives. Mother Ann's charismatic personality attracted radical pietists seeking direct evidence, authority, and assurance that they were on the road to ultimate Truth. She claimed that the Godhead dwelt in her, and her followers implied that she was in fact the female reincarnation of Christ. She seemed to have superhuman powers of prophecy and to be able to perform miracles of healing. At the same time, the celibate, ascetic, and communal aspects of her sect seemed very much in harmony with the austere simplicity and brotherhood of primitive Christianity. Perhaps also Mother Ann's emphasis upon the sinfulness of human passion and lust, and the peculiar dancing ceremonies with their ecstatic twirlings and fallings, provided a psychological escape from some of the repressive rigors of New England Puritanism. Mother Ann promised her followers complete peace and assurance of salvation within her church and nowhere else. A ritual of confession also helped the new convert purge himself of secret sins and bound him to his new brethren.

Backus heard of this new delusion and made a trip to Pittsfield in 1782 to investigate. He stayed with Elder Valentine Rathbun, one of the leading Baptists of the vicinity, who himself had been briefly "ensnared" in the movement in 1780 but who had left it after three months. Rathbun's vitriolic exposure of the sect accused Mother Ann of being a hypocrite and an alcoholic and her followers of being charlatans. He had in fact become so fanatical in his hatred of "those people called Shakers" that he urged the authorities of Pittsfield to drive them out of town.

When Backus arrived, two of Rathbun's brothers, one of his brothers-in-law, and four of his adult children were still living among the Shakers. Backus spent four hours arguing with Daniel Rathbun and then visited some of the Shakers who "appeared loving & mild as long as we would hear them with attention, but when we endeavoured to hold up light against them, they were all noise and confusion." Backus concluded that the sect was totally disreputable and Mother Ann nothing but "a common prostitute."

A year later a Shaker itinerant named Stephen Williams came to southeastern Massachusetts and preached in the town of Raynham adjoining Middleborough. Backus went over to meet Williams and refute him. He summarized the Shaker views under five headings: "Those Shakers evidently are like the papists in the following points: 1. In holding an earthly head to their church. 2. That out of it is no salvation. 3. That none can enter into it but by confessing their sins to a creature. 4. That they must implicitly believe and do as their leaders say. 5. That the way of salvation is, do and live." In 1784 he wrote of them, "their chief leaders delight themselves much in feasting and drinking spiritous liquor. . . . They endeavor to enforce and propagate their scheme with a strange power, signs, and lying wonders. Some of them at Norton and elsewhere have carried matters so far this year as for men and women to dance together entirely naked, to imitate the primitive state of perfection. And their forcibly stripping a woman of one of their families, who testified against their wickedness, has moved the authority of Bristol county lately to take them in hand therefore." Backus also reported that "a motion was made in our legislature to have them punished by authority, which motion was negatived by the majority of a single vote." He left no doubt that he regretted the failure of the motion. President Manning of the Baptist college was equally hostile in reporting, in 1783, that "they pretend to talk in unknown tongues" and "Some carnal fruits . . . have inadvertently resulted from their chaste embraces." While the people of New England were generally hostile to the Shakers, who were several times driven out of towns by mobs, the Baptists were the most vehement and the least tolerant. Ezra Stiles explained in 1786 that the Shakers were "almost to a man" converts from the Separate-Baptists. However, the Shaker threat proved short-lived. Mother Ann died in 1784 and the movement went into temporary quiescence for twenty years. Backus reported in 1795, "we seldom hear of them now."

Backus also had to fight off a countervailing pull toward hyper-Calvinism in "the New Divinity" stimulated by pupils of Edwards. Its prime exponent was Samuel Hopkins, the Congregational minister of Newport; other important figures included Nathaniel Emmons, Joseph Bellamy, and Jonathan Edwards, Jr. These men tried to carry Edwards's rejection of the pre-Awakening view of the covenant theology to its logical extreme, and to erect in its place "Consistent Calvinism"—a system which to the lay mind seemed to advocate outright determinism or, in eighteenth century terms, "fatalism." They stated so flatly the impossibility of man's doing anything to obtain salvation that their common proof of regeneration was "a willingness to be damned for the glory of God."

The New Divinity appalled Backus as a gross perversion of the thinking of the great Edwards. Nathaniel Emmons, he wrote in his diary in 1785, "has carried the doctrine of predestination so far as to insist that God positively produces or creates sin; a shocking error!" The "Hopkintonians" thought they were simply following out Edwards's claim that "The will is always determined by the strongest motive." Since the strongest motives in depraved human nature were selfish and sinful, men always or "inevitably" acted wrongly.

Backus denied the legitimacy of their connection with Edwards. "I am much better acquainted with Edwards's writing than they are." His tract, *The Sovereign Decrees of God* (1773) denied the propriety of using "the word 'inevitable' concerning the reprobate and 'irresistible' concerning the elect in such a manner as to exclude the idea of their own choice." To do so put the whole obligation of salvation upon God. God had created the fundamental laws of the universe, but he was not responsible for all their consequences; God had created man a free or morally responsible agent. If the Unitarians, Universalists, and Freewillers erred in making man too important in his salvation, the neo-Edwardsians or Hopkinsians erred in denying man any part in his salvation. "The means of grace are calculated in infinite wisdom to open the eyes of men, and to turn them from darkness to light, and from the power of Satan unto God. Precepts and promises, rewards and punishments, calls and warnings, are all motives to influence the choice of man. And the strongest hold that the devil has in this world is to persuade man, that a being governed in his choice by motives without himself, is inconsistent with the liberty of moral agents; and to persuade him at the same time that necessity obliges God to pardon and save them, whenever they shall become sincere penitents. Thus they assume a sovereignty to themselves which they deny to their Maker." For men to say fatalistically, "if we are entirely dependent upon the sovereign will of God for . . . grace, then all our use of means to attain salvation is vain" was as foolish as to say that if God wants us to live he would send us manna and clothes from heaven and we need not work.

While there was little danger that many Baptists would be persuaded to rejoin the Standing churches, there was some danger that the neo-Edwardseans might persuade some Baptist ministers to adopt their approach. In 1776, for example, Elder Noah Alden of Bellingham was complained of by his church for implying that he was preaching only for the elect, just as many Standing ministers were accused of doing. He seemed to believe, as the neo-Edwardseans did, that sinners could not act from proper motives and therefore it was idle to try to call them to repentance or even to urge them to prayer. The council called to bring Alden to task for his views accepted his explanation that he thought it proper "to preach the law closely to sinners" but "could not in direct terms invite them" to accept the gospel. Other Baptist elders did, however, preach the "consistent Calvinism" of the New Divinity in these years; and it is probable that disgruntled laymen from their churches joined the Universalists, Shakers, Freewillers, and Methodists.

As a defender of the faith Backus also wrote tracts emphasizing the importance of baptism by immersion, the internal call to preach, the liberal support of gospel ministers, family prayer, congregational autonomy, and strict discipline for the maintenance of a pure church of gathered saints. And in every tract he stressed the errors of infant baptism. In an ordination sermon delivered in 1772, Backus defined the role of evangelical ministers. "A principal part of their work" was "to labour to reconcile sinners to God." But Backus insisted on the pastoral function as well—the strengthening of the faith of the saints, the inculcation of doctrinal truth, the expounding of moral and ethical truth, and the general care of souls and bodies which had always been the duties of the pastor of a parish. In striving to distinguish between the errors of cold formality in Old Light, Arminian preachers, and of arid legalism in hyper-Calvinist preachers in the Standing Order, Backus laid great stress upon the rightful evangelistic aspects of the New Light ministers. Thus a shift in the role of the minister became inevitable. Given the New Light assumptions concerning the fundamental necessity of a conversion experience and of the lively preaching of the Word as the principal "means of grace" in "the divine economy of things," no function was more important than evangelism.

Backus remained an optimist. Just as Jefferson thought that by 1830 the whole nation would turn Unitarian in the triumph of reason over superstition, Backus fully expected that by that date the whole nation would be immersed, evangelical Baptists. The American Revolution was an act of God which foretold "the advancement and completion of the Redeemer's kingdom." The worldly man might attribute the successful Revolution to a mere triumph for political liberty, but the Christian recognized it "as one more important step towards bringing in the glory of the latter day." The millennial hope which had made Massachusetts Bay seem like "a city set upon a hill," and which made Jonathan Edwards see the Great Awakening as the inauguration of the Second Coming, filled the Separate-Baptists with the conviction that the new American nation was itself the hope of the world: "Nor is it at all improbable," said the Warren Association in 1784, "that America is reserved in the mind of Jehovah to be the grand theatre on which the divine Redeemer will accomplish glorious things. . . . If we observe the signs of the times, we shall find reason to think he is on his way."

Yet there was another side to the mind of Isaac Backus. His pietism was not anti-intellectual except in preferring the Christian virtues to "mere intellect," the perceptions of the heart to those of the head. "Let none think me an Enemy to Learning," he wrote in his first published tract in 1754, "for true Learning is what I highly prize." Truly learning inevitably brought men closer to God. He never fully comprehended the ultimate implications of Lockean and Newtonian thought, and what he took from them he circumscribed within the narrow framework of evangelical Calvinism. Nevertheless, he looked forward rather than backward; he tried to open the religious thought and practice of his day to the new science, and he did not seek to escape the impact of the Age of Reason. In many ways he displayed a striking sensibility to the new scientific, empirical, and pragmatic way of looking at things. Always ready to learn by the trial and error of the experimental method, he had a favorite phrase for it: "we experimentally saw" what would work.

For example, Backus saw the importance of annual statistics of the growth of the denomination as a means of convincing politicians that the sect must be reckoned with. He encouraged the collection of such statistics, and took every occasion to check their accuracy and then to publish them. The same concern for tabulating, comparing, categorizing, and measuring was evident in his diaries, travel journals, and manuscripts. For sixty years he kept a manuscript entitled "Bills of Mortality" in which he listed all of the deaths in Middleborough and vicinity and also examples of extraordinary events relating to death or accidents—particularly plagues and epidemics. He kept another list of all of the ordination dates (with biographical data) of every Separate and Separate-Baptist minister in New England. He kept a list of every book he purchased and added to his library. He wrote a genealogical history of both his father's and his mother's families, going back to the earliest settlers in America. He kept detailed notebooks with entries for all of his business dealings for his farm, book-selling, his iron-trading, and his day-to-day costs for food, clothes, travel, and household items. He made a separate list with every horse he ever purchased. His church records were equally full, detailed, and accurate. And he kept careful notes and extracts from all that he read. In this concern Backus shared the Enlightenment view that through the careful observation and collection of facts man could learn to know the world in which he lived. God worked according to established laws both in the spiritual and in the natural world; what seemed acts of wonder and awe, miracles or providential accidents were really part of a master plan which might be fathomed if sufficient data were collected about it.

The seventeenth century Puritans tended to react immediately in terms of mystery and wonder to what they saw. The eighteenth century produced a greater willingness for suspending judgment pending further investigation and experience. Backus shared with Cotton Mather the belief that plagues and epidemics were not simply to be submitted to as judgments of God if He had also provided a means whereby men could save themselves from these "natural" ills. In 1778 Backus took his whole family to be inoculated for smallpox in a small temporary hospital set up for this purpose on the outskirts of Bridgewater. He did

so in spite of the insistence of his friend, Elder Peleg Bur-
roughs of the Baptist Church in Dartmouth, that inoculation was contrary to Scripture because God had said,
"They that be whole need not a physician but they that
are sick"—Matthew 9:12. In his diary Backus made a detailed record of the progress of the disease from the inoculation of the live virus to the cure, listing even the number
of pocks on the bodies of each member of his family.

He sometimes speculated as to whether epidemics and
plagues were visitations from God to display His anger
or to awaken people to their sinfulness. But often he simply recorded them as acts of nature without comment. He
took a great interest in the effectiveness of inoculation
and recorded in his diary that when Boston underwent a
bad siege of the smallpox in 1792, 9,374 persons had the
disease; out of 232 persons who had it but were not inoculated 33 died (or 14 percent) but out of 9,152 who were
inoculated only 165 (or 2 percent) died.

Backus was similarly ambivalent toward the earth-
quakes which shook New England in the 1750's. He attempted to record the details precisely, but the lack of
any known prevention for them and their magnitude led
him to speculate about their supernatural significance.
"I was waked up with the shock of an Earthquake," he
wrote on November 17, 1755, "which rock'd the house and
the bed I lay in like a Cradle; the Shaking continu'd Some
minutes and then the roaring noise of it was heard some
time after. Such a season I never knew before, which put
me in mind of the dissolution of all things." Four days
later, on his way to Cape Cod, he recorded some of the
strange occurrences which seemed to be connected with
this event: "I find many tokens of destroying times ap-
proaching. . . . I have on this journey had direct information that lately a Woman at Bilinsget [Billingsgate]
made some Bread, one at Yarmouth a Stupye [stew pie]
another at Barnstable some dumpling and a fourth at

Harwich a pudding, that all appear'd like as if they were mingled with blood, which they could give no natural cause for." Backus recorded the story with obvious credulity, yet he had taken the trouble to inquire for "natural causes."

At other times Backus was capable of recording a strange phenomenon with clinical objectivity, offering a purely natural explanation for its occurrence.

Mr. Nicholas Wade of Bridgr. near the border of Halifax, had a sheep which seem'd to swell till she could not go nor stand, and at last died on the 17th instant; and next morning he cut her open, when to his great surprise there came out a thing that had some features of a lamb, but much more of a negro female child. It was larger than a middling child is at its birth, was 10 inches broad across the breast and shoulders, its back and thighs shaped like a child and smooth all over except a woolly hair upon its head. Great numbers of peple flockt to see it and dr. Isaac Otis dissected it and found that inwardly as well as outwardly it had more resemblance to a child than a beast, and tis suspected to be the effect of beastiality of a Negro in the neighbourhood. Such an awful instance I have not heard of in my day before.

Still it would be erroneous to portray Backus as a man of the Enlightenment in any profound sense. He was not really interested in science and his preoccupation with the reality and direct manifestations of divinity in revivals and conversions predisposed him to favor supernatural explanations for peculiar events. There is even evidence that he still retained a belief in witchcraft, for the power of the devil was as real to him as the power of God:

August 3, 1789: Preacht at John McFarleon's in Pembroke, whose son Seth hath been thought to be bewitched, till the night after July 24, when he says a voice informed him that the ghost that appeared to him [some days ago] was from Halifax, Nova Scotia, where he was last winter and [where] he helped to release a woman from two robbers; but that she is since dead and now [her ghost] came to compel him to go there to be a witness against them and accordingly he set off the 27th [for Nova Scotia].

The list Backus kept of his library, and the surviving volumes with his name, reveal that he was not well-read in the works of the Enlightenment. He received a copy of Alexander Pope's *Essay on Man* as a gift from his friend John Davis in 1772. He took notes on Beccaria's *Essay on Crime and Punishment* in 1789. He had read Locke's essays on government, toleration, and *On the Understanding*. But by and large his library consisted of polemical and exegetical works relating to the current theological and practical problems of the churches in his day. It was well stocked with the volumes of English Baptists like Bunyan, Norcott, Gill, Stennett, Wallin, and Crosby. It had most of the important writings of the Separates like Frothingham, Paine, and Holly, and the attacks on them by Fish, Lord, and Chauncy. Backus read widely in the books of English and American Congregationalists like Watts, Doddridge, and Owen, Bellamy, Emmons, and Hopkins; and he owned Milton's *Paradise Lost* and the historical works of Suetonius, Knox, Rapid, Crosby, Gordon, and Hutchinson. He knew thoroughly the seventeenth century works of American Puritans like John Cotton and the Mathers and the answers to them by John Robinson and Roger Williams. He also bought the works of Whitefield and Thomas Prince on the Awakening. But there is no evidence of reading in the realms of science, philosophy, or mathematics.

As a historian, however, he was a man of the Enlightenment. His four volumes on the history of New England "with particular reference to the Baptists," were thoroughly and carefully documented. Backus was forced to rely almost entirely upon primary sources for his mate-

rial. He devoted an amazing amount of time to reading over lengthy theological works, poring over the old
court records, church records, legislative archives, and
private papers which he found in Massachusetts, Connecticut, and Rhode Island. Moreover, he enlisted the aid of
other Baptists to send him copies of old letters, diaries,
church minutes, petitions, sermons, tracts, and pamphlets. From these sources he quoted liberally in his volumes.
So solid was his history despite his own obvious bias that
no serious challenge to its accuracy was ever made. To this
day it remains one of the great source books for Colonial
history.

Backus displayed his regard for factual accuracy in other
ways. A thirty-two page letter to Jedidiah Morse on March
9, 1791, pointed out many errors of fact and interpretation
in the first major edition of *American Geography*.
Though there is no record that Morse ever acknowledged
these comments, later editions of his geography incorporated most of the corrections. Backus's three contributions
to the Massachusetts Historical Society, all in the volume
of collections for 1794, were in keeping with the publications of the society. None contained any hint that Backus
was a Baptist or pietist. They were strictly factual and
"scientific." It seems likely that through them Backus
was making a serious bid to be admitted as a member of
this learned society. But no invitation to join it ever came.

To the members of the Standing Order who controlled the Massachusetts Historical Society (most of
them Unitarians) Backus always remained an outsider, a
benighted defender of a bizarre faith. But if he failed to
achieve recognition as a writer or thinker, there was one
matter on which the Standing Order anxiously sought his
help at this time: they wanted him to aid the federalists in
establishing the new national constitution.

VIII

Critical Years for the New American Nation

1780–1790

"With what a surprising progress have we stepped up to our present importance and rank amongst the nations." Warren Baptist Association, *Minutes* (1784)

THE BAPTISTS shared the general euphoric optimism of Americans in believing that God had chosen them for an important role in the destiny of man. But for Backus the 1780's were "the critical period" in American history. His day-to-day assessment of the crisis in his diary was often in stark contrast with his long-range hopes. The brief summation of the year 1783 neatly epitomized the balance between his hopes and fears. "Great indeed have been the events of this year. The British Court gave up her claims of power over the American States. . . . In the meantime the great men of the earth crowded in their fine wares upon us, which all ranks of people in America were fond of buying, to our unspeakable damage, in the sinking of public credit, and the most extravagant gratification of pride, intemperance, fraud and cruel oppres-

sion." The entry concluded with the text, Revelations
18:23: "And the light of a candle shall shine no more at
all in thee; and the voice of the bridegroom and of the
bride shall be heard no more at all in thee; for thy merchants were the great men of the earth; for by thy sor-
ceries were all nations deceived."

Similar gloomy statements summed up his diaries
throughout the next five or six years. Like Jeremiah he
lamented the "profaneness, cruel oppression, damnable
heresies, and a dead sleep about religion" which prevailed
throughout the land. A climactic pitch was reached in the
turmoil surrounding Shays's Rebellion in 1786. That year
Backus published a tract entitled *The Testimony of the
Two Witnesses,* an apocalyptic exegesis of Revelations
11:3. Backus sought to describe how America had entered
into a critical period and what it must do to emerge from
it. "Our late most cruel war" he blamed upon the designing bishops of the Church of England, who wished to
spread episcopacy to America, and who encouraged Parliament to force the colonies to submit to its full authority.
He compared the German mercenaries to "the beast which
John saw" pursuing him in Revelations. "Yet this bloody
chace was no sooner over than the merchants of Babylon
[London], even the great men of the earth, filled this
country with her splendid and costly wares; by means of
which public credit . . . has been bought and sold for a
trifle. And the spirit of pride and luxury like Sodom . . .
has prevailed amazingly." This was written on June 16,
1786, and Backus seemed at this time inclined to sympathize more with the debtors than with the creditors of
the new nation: "public and private debts are demanded
with great rigour as if brick could be made without straw."

Two months later the debtors of Massachusetts began
holding conventions to protest against the "cruel oppression" which Backus described, and in September the

uprising led by Shays, Job Shattuck, and Luke Day began. For five months Massachusetts faced incipient civil war as Shays and Day led bands of destitute farmers, former Revolutionary soldiers, about the countryside intimidating the county courts which were settling suits in favor of the creditors. Shays was finally defeated on February 4, 1787, after a brief encounter, and the rebellion came to an abrupt end.

Armed uprising shocked Backus. Six weeks after Shays's defeat he wrote *An Address to the Inhabitants of New-England Concerning the Present Bloody Controversy Therein.* Here he took the side of the government and opposed the demand of the farmers for more paper money with which to pay off their taxes, mortgages, and other debts. "The scarcity of money" was "owing to our own folly." "Immense sums" were expended "for the gewgaws imported from Europe, and the more pernicious produce of the West Indies [rum]." Backus concurred with the view "that a paper currency would produce calamities without end." "Without a reformation of manners we can have little hope to prosper in our publick or private concerns." His tract enjoined all citizens to remember "the Command of God is 'Submit yourselves to every ordinance of man for the Lord's sake.'" Backus and the Baptists were not alienated from their society; they had a stake in the existing system, for all its shortcomings. And they looked askance at those who sought to overturn it by violent means. Backus was willing to criticize the merchants, the lawyers, the oppressors of the poor, but he was not ready to condone rebellion. Like the legislature, he believed that the fault lay as much with the folly and greed of the farmers as it did with the creditors who wanted to collect honest debts.

The zeal of the Revolution in the United States never reached the pitch it did in France because of the evangelical temper which dominated the new nation. Evangelicals like Backus believed that reform must begin with the individual. "A reformation of manners" and morals was the proper solution to the critical economic and political problems facing the state of Massachusetts—not more revolution. The Baptists did not agree with Jefferson that a little revolution now and then was a good thing.

The Baptists also demonstrated their conservative temper by their general coolness toward the new federal Constitution. Any move toward a stronger central government was, like any move toward presbyterian or episcopal polity in religion, a threat to the freedom of the individual and to local home rule. Middleborough was badly split on the issue of ratification of the Constitution drawn up in Philadelphia in 1787. Backus no doubt shared the prevailing Baptist view against it. He was one of the four delegates Middleborough sent to the convention which met in Boston in January, 1788, to consider the question of ratifying the new Constitution. This was the only office to which the town ever elected Backus, and it was a signal mark of the respect in which his neighbors held him.

The best political estimate indicated that 192 delegates opposed ratification and only 144 favored it. The leading politicians in the state, including John Hancock and Samuel Adams, were either opposed or undecided. The votes of the twenty Baptists in the convention might be crucial. James Manning was therefore induced to come to Boston as an observer by some leading Federalists, for it was well known that he favored ratification. Samuel Stillman, himself a delegate from Boston, also supported ratification. If he and Manning could win Backus to their side, these three leading men might carry the twenty Baptist votes in a bloc for federalism.

Backus's reflections reveal his attitude. He understood

the reasoning of James Wilson, one of the framers, who had argued that a new constitution was needed: " 'The evil has stolen in from a quarter little suspected, and the rock of Freedom, which stood firm against the attacks of a foreign foe, has been sapped and undermined by the licentiousness of our own citizens. The commencement of peace was likewise the commencement of our distress and disgrace. Devoid of power, we could neither prevent the excessive importations which lately deluged the country nor even raise from the excess a contribution to the public revenue.' " But Backus noted that Wilson argued there was a power in all government "from which there is no appeal." "Which power," Backus commented, "he says is in the people, and he would have them give a large measure of it to the new Congress." Backus was dubious, for the people had created a new constitution in Massachusetts which violated the religious rights of the Baptists.

Backus was pleased to find at the convention that "each delegate had full liberty in his turn to say all he pleased, for or against the Constitution; by means of which I obtained much more light about the extensive affairs of our Country, the nature of the proposed Constitution, and the security of the rights of the people therein, than I had when I went from home." In short, the debates took him out of his parochial view of the issues at stake and also modified some of his doubts about the threat of majority tyranny. Here as elsewhere the Baptists of New England displayed a distrust of democracy almost as great as their dislike for monarchy or aristocracy, especially when the masses were unwashed in the blood of the Lamb.

On January 19, after he had been listening to the debates for four days, Backus was invited to dine with Governor James Bowdoin, along with two other Baptist elders, Noah Alden of Bellingham and Valentine Rathbun of Pittsfield. The Governor then no doubt tried to persuade his guests of the virtues of the new constitution so that they might use their influence with the other Baptist delegates. On January 20, a Sabbath, Backus heard President Manning preach in the morning and Noah Alden in the afternoon. He himself preached in the evening at Elder Stillman's house "to a large audience." In the next few days he also dined with other important gentlemen, leading figures in the state, and all ardent supporters of ratification.

On February 1 he concluded that the final decision would be in favor of the Constitution, with a recommendation of some amendments which would "be for the best upon the whole." He had decided to support ratification, though not with any great enthusiasm. He did not, however, dare to return home until the final vote: "It is very disagreeable to be detained here so long, and not to have been able to send any supply to our people," he wrote to his wife; "but I can't think it advisable to leave the Convention until the great point is turned which is of vast importance."

Having made up his mind that ratification was desirable, Backus decided to speak for it. He was the first Baptist to do so. On February 4 he spoke of "the great advantage of having religious tests and hereditary nobility excluded from our government." These two items in the Constitution seemed to him a guarantee against any establishment of religion and against the formation of any aristocracy. "Some serious minds discover a concern lest, if all religious tests should be excluded, the congress would hereafter establish Popery, or some other tyrannical way of worship. But it is most certain that no such way of worship can be established without any religious test." He said "Popery," but he probably feared, as many Baptists did, that some form of Calvinism of the Presbyterian or Consociational variety was more likely. His interpretation of this article helps to explain why the Baptists made no effort to fight for an amendment on freedom of religion along with the others which the convention sent to Congress.

Backus commended in his speech the clause "excluding all titles of nobility, or hereditary succession of power" on the grounds that "the American revolution was built upon the principle, that all men are born with an equal right to liberty and property, and that officers have no right to any power but what is fairly given them by the consent of the people." He also mentioned the abolition of the slave trade. Several members of his family, including his father and his brother Elijah, had owned slaves and there is no indication that he ever protested against slavery before 1788. Nor did he here speak out for the abolition of slavery itself. But he did make clear his own dislike for the system and his antipathy toward trafficking in human merchandise. Some at the convention had complained that the Constitution did not abolish slavery outright, as the people of Massachusetts had done. Backus could not agree with them: "no man abhors that wicked practice more than I do, and would gladly make use of all lawful means towards the abolishing of slavery in all parts of the land. But let us consider where we are and what we are doing. In the articles of confederation no provision was made to hinder the importing of slaves into any of these states; but a door is now open hereafter to do it, and each state is at liberty now to abolish slavery as soon as they please. . . . slavery grows more and more odious through the world; and as an honorable gentleman said [here] some days ago, 'Though we cannot say that slavery is struck with an apoplexy, yet we may hope it will die with a consumption.' " He concluded that the Constitution gave the government power to end the slave trade, but that the abolition of slavery must be left up to each state. His speech relied on the Bible, whose revealed truths he tried to reconcile with the natural rights philosophy of the Constitution.

"Earnest attempts" to adjourn the convention without taking action on the Constitution, he wrote, "did not obtain." On February 6 the advocates of ratification succeeded in their plan for adopting the Constitution with recommended amendments. "About sun down the grand question was put, upon which there were 187 yeas and 168 nays; so that the Constitution was establish'd by a majority of 19." Yet neither his influence, nor that of Manning or Stillman, had persuaded "the country members" who were Baptists. "Elder Alden of Bellingham, elder Rathbun of Pittsfield, elder Tingley of Waterborough (county of York) all voted against it, and so did two thirds of the baptist members of the Convention of which there were above twenty. Elder Stillman and I, with twelve congregational ministers, voted for it; though doubtless with very different motives."

President Manning was as shocked by the negative attitude of the Baptist delegates as Backus. He "considered Massachusetts the hinge on which the whole must turn" and was "mortified to find Father [Noah] Alden among the *nays*." Manning and Backus might have taken some credit, however, for having swung about seven Baptists into the "ayes." Backus received £3 in pay and "paid off my reckonings, viz. £2.6.6 for boarding at capt. Samuel Daggetts 23 days. 2/2 for washing linen, 9/4 to mr. Sherburn for keeping my hourse 7 nights, and 2/4 to a Barber for shaving &c. 7 times; in all £3.0.4." He had nothing left over to buy anything for his wife as he had hoped. "I came home that night to mr. Seth Mann's; and the 9th. came home: found that my daughter Sibel hath wasted in her flesh considerably in my absence."

His vote in the convention did not endear Backus to his

congregation. The Sunday after he returned he "preacht twice to our people, tho' some are very uneasy at my voting for the New Constitution." Of the four delegates from Middleborough, two had voted against it and one joined Backus in favor. One of the opponents, Isaac Soule, organized a convention to oppose the new Constitution in May, 1788, but nothing came of it. A month later, when Backus was passing through Methuen, he lodged with the deacon of the Baptist church there and noted that he "Had a conference, at the request of many, about our federal Constitution of government." The Baptists must have considered Backus something of a traitor to his group for the stand he took. How else could they explain the fact that he and Stillman (a well known conservative city pastor) were on the same side as their "enemies," the Standing ministers, and against all of their country brethren?

On his return Backus also faced a personal tragedy. His daughter was seriously ill, probably with cancer. For six weeks he watched in sadness as she slowly grew worse. On March 23 he entered this account of her sickness in his diary: "My daughter Sibel hath gradually declined until she was scarce able to sit up today. And she wasted away fast, with ulcers or putrefaction in her stomach and bowels, which caused much pain; yet we never heard a murmering word from her mouth. She had a very deep sense of sin upon her mind, and distressing fears that she had not true conviction, because her heart was so vile and hard. She once requested us to pray that she might have such a clear sight of Gods righteousness as to give us her all into his hands. At another time I asked her if she had such a view of a righteous and gracious God as to be willing to give up her soul and all into his hands? Her answer was, 'I think I have.' And she give a like answer to a like question a few hours before her decease, which was on Lordsday M[a]r. 23, about half after four o'clock afternoon. I preacht twice and then came and saw my dear daughter pass through the dark valy, without such a manifestation of light as I longed for, which grieved my heart. But God is wise and righteous, and hath done us no wrong. So far from it, that he hath given us for 20 years, her life and her useful labours for the most of that time, in such an obedient manner as scarce ever to need a reproof from us. A great privilege!" To see his youngest daughter die at twenty was hard enough; but to believe that she died without conversion and would never be re-united with him and his wife in heaven was the most painful of all griefs to a pietist.

Three weeks later his daughter Lucy married Alpheus Fobes and moved to Bridgewater: "thus two are gone out of our family lately." Backus must have begun to feel the loneliness of old age. He was now over sixty-four and did not know that he still had eighteen active years before him. Six months after Sibel's death he undertook the longest and most laborious evangelistic tour of his career.

It had its origin at the annual meeting of the Warren Association which began on September 6, 1788. Backus laid before this meeting a proposal for a "memorial and petition for the full establishment of religious liberty, directed to our General Court." The time was ripe for a renewed attack upon the established system, he said. "They [the Standing Order] may now do it with honor. Nothing is so honorable in man as to act consistently and honestly. And though the exercise of a commanding power in religious matters might appear so, as long as religious tests were required of all who came into office, yet now, when all such tests are to be excluded [in the federal constitution], it certainly must be agreeable to consistency and honesty to leave the command over ministers and churches in the direction and support of worship entirely to our Lord Jesus Christ." His belief that the Constitution of the United States had prohibited any establishment of religion by its clause against religious tests for officeholders led him to think that the Standing Order in New England would align its own system with the national policy by abandoning compulsory religious taxes.

The delegates to the Warren Association sensed that Backus had misjudged the political climate in New England and the temper and mood of the denomination. His proposal was approved only "after some debate" and a committee was instructed "to present this, or a similar petition in such time and manner as they shall think proper." The committee, dominated by conservative Baptists, decided that the time was not ripe. The incident was symbolic both of the waning interest among the Baptists in political action and of the waning of Backus's influence with the denomination on this score. The new generation of Baptists, which had not gone through the sufferings of the early days of the movement, was more interested in increasing the size and prestige of the denomination than in antagonizing the Standing Order. The militant cries of an old warhorse sounded on deaf ears.

But as if to mollify Backus and to turn his talents to other uses, the Association nominated him for a more important task. A letter had been read from the "General Committee composed of the Delegates who represent the several Baptist Associations in Virginia." It reported that a great revival was taking place among the Southern Baptists as a result of a union of various factions within the denomination which had been at odds for the past forty years—the Regular Baptists, the Separate Baptists, and the Independent Baptists. God had immediately showered upon this unity a multitude of blessings. The revival was in fact so great that the Southern Baptists asked the Warren Association to send some ministers down to help garner the harvest of waiting souls.

"This information was confirmed by a pleasing verbal

account from Rev. Mr. [Asa] Hunt who visited that country [Virginia] the last winter and had opportunity of
seeing the wonderful displays of grace upon large numbers who are hopefully brought to an acquaintance with the
gospel." Hunt was pastor of the Third Baptist Church in
Middleborough and a close friend of Backus's, whom he
had already told of the great "work of God" in Virginia.
The Warren Association nominated Backus and Hunt, by
"a general voice," to go to Virginia to assist in the work.
"This," wrote Backus in his diary, "was entirely unex-
pected; but I agreed to take it into consideration and act
as light should be given." By November 19 he had made up
his mind to go and made arrangements to sail from Newport with Capt. Daggett of Boston. The ship was to leave in
mid-December. Backus was about to participate in the
beginning of the Second Great Awakening in America.

Unable to get a ship for Virginia, he landed instead in
Beaufort County, North Carolina. For the next five
months he traveled through that state and Virginia,
preaching almost daily and meeting all of the leading Baptists. He had two principal purposes in view: to build
up the churches in the area and to cement the ties between
the Northern and Southern wings of the denomination.
Links between the Baptists of the two regions already ex-
isted as the result of itinerant evangelism of New England
Separate-Baptists like Shubael Stearns and Daniel Mar-
shall since the 1750's and John Leland since 1776. While
there had been considerable rivalry between the Arminian
Baptists already on the scene and the newcomers, who
were Regular or Separate Baptists, all three groups grew
rapidly during the next forty years, as the Anglican
church steadily declined in vitality. Backus described its
ministers as principally "drunkards, card-players and
swearers." He later told his brother Elijah in Connecticut,
"Before 1768 there were but 5 Baptist churches" in Vir-

ginia "and now they have more than an hundred churches, some of which have 5 or 600 members."

While New Light Presbyterians, led by Samuel Davies, had captured many of the better-educated and more prosperous people in the eastern part of the state, the Baptists swayed the middle and lower classes; the Methodists just beginning to overcome the stigma of being Tories and Anglicans were starting to compete with both. Backus found newly formed Baptist congregations everywhere, but so few elders to preach to them that most were trying to be pastors simultaneously to three or four churches. As in New England, the Baptists were itinerant circuit riders from the beginning. Backus also found many parts of these states without any religious life at all. "Irreligion hath prevailed so far in this country, & its civil effects are so plainly felt, that many appear sensable of the want of religious influence to promote their civil welfare, and the baptists are as much, if not the most esteemed of any religious denomination. Oh, that New England knew the worth of their privileges & would thankfully improve them!" It was a revelation to him to discover that many of the ruling elite in North Carolina and Virginia had joined the Baptist churches and that there was no stigma whatever attached to the denomination.

Typical of the prominent Baptists he met were Colonel Thomas Read, "a wealthy and very prominent citizen of Charlotte County;" Eleazar Clay of Chesterfield County, the uncle of Henry Clay and reputedly worth $100,000; and Councilor Robert Carter of Nomini Hall, a man who had often sat as a member of the Governor's council and who was one of the most influential men in Virginia. Carter owned over 500 slaves, and Backus found that almost every Baptist he met owned several. Carter caused a great stir in 1791 when he decided to free his slaves; and John Leland, the most radical Baptist elder in the South, found no one to support his resolution in 1790 when he persuaded the General Committee of the Baptist Associations to endorse abolition. By and large the Baptists Backus met in the South had no interest in putting an end to slavery, though they did take an interest in saving the souls of the bondsmen. Backus attended an association meeting in Virginia which discussed questions like the following: "What should be done when a man slave was owned by one master and his wife by another, and one was carried to such a distance as never to be likely to see the other in this world? Whether they must continue single or not? Also whether a master or mistress had a right to correct servants who were members of the same church for family disobedience?" The Southern Baptists seem to have been frustrated by the attempt to maintain their conceptions of moral and ecclesiastical order in the face of a system which denied both Christian and civil rights to Negroes. Asked for his opinion on these disturbing matters, Backus "gave the best light" he had. But he felt no call to rebuke his brethren or strike out, as Leland did, against the system. He still hoped that this "wicked practice" would die with some providential "consumption."

His tour of the South was physically tiring but spiritually invigorating. "I could hardly be willing to tarry so long from my dear family and people [his congregation]" he wrote to his wife on March 9, 1789; "Yet when I view a vast field for labour, and no prospect of ever being in it again, and that a main design of my coming cannot be answered without staying [to meet the General Committee], and that thereby much good may likely be done, the clearest light is to stay & to return the first opportunity afterwards." He felt particularly anxious to help his Southern brethren fight off the dangers of the Methodists; "To hold up light against their errors, and others, is of great importance at this time when many have an ear to hear; and I hope the above consideration will satesfy you & our people. . . ." A week later he wrote again, "The Methodists have done much to hinder the work, but their influence is greatly lessened." He feared the doctrinal errors of this new sect, which "sprang from the church of England" and he suspected it was "trying hard for power" in civil affairs. The fact that the Methodists had an episcopal polity and had not fought with the Baptists for disestablishment in Virginia increased these fears. Though Backus and his friends made fun of the emotionalism and disorder of Methodist revival meetings, the Baptist revivals were just as full of enthusiasm. Southern evangelical pietism, as the camp meetings were soon to reveal, far outstripped the First Great Awakening in emotional excesses. Before he died Backus received many letters from evangelists he met on this trip who had moved westward to Tennessee and Kentucky and took part in the religious orgies of the frontier.

At the end of May Backus boarded a ship in Norfolk for New York. He stopped in that city from June 5 to 9 to preach at Elder Benjamin Foster's Baptist church about the great work of God in Virginia. On June 8 he attended the meetings of the first federal Congress, where he sat in the gallery "and heard Mr. [James] Madison and others speak" about the First Amendment. On June 9 he boarded another ship and arrived home on June 18. He summarized the trip briefly in his diary: "Between Jan. 10 and May 27 I travelled in North-Carolina and Virginia 1251 miles and preacht 117 sermons, generally to people who were very earnest to hear the word. The church of England, which was supported by law till the late war, is now fallen into contempt, and the law to support their ministers by tax has been repealed above 3 years; and the baptists are in the best credit with their rulers of any denomination in Virginia as well as North Carolina. O,

what hath God wrought!" He had traveled in all, by land
and sea, 2620 miles, "The greatest journey I ever went."

The final act of his trip was to report to the Warren
Association at its annual meeting in September, 1789,
on his journey to the South, "where the Lord hath been
pleased to make remarkable displays of his power and
grace in the conversion of large numbers." It was a great
sadness to him that the Baptists of New England did not
seem to be experiencing a similar revival at this time.
During the last years of his life he turned his attention to
an effort to promote such a movement.

IX

Elder Statesman
of the Baptists
1790–1806

---

*"The liberty that he [Roger Williams] was for,
civil and religious, is now enjoyed in thirteen of
the seventeen of the United States of America. No
tax for any religious minister is imposed by authority in any of the said thirteen States, and their
power is much weakened in the other four."* ISAAC
BACKUS, ms. letter to William Richards, August 20,
1805

IN MANY RESPECTS the 1790's seemed to Backus
as critical as the preceding decade; he often wondered
whether God was not about to chastize the new nation for its stubborn reluctance to see the New Light. The
failure of the revival spirit of the Virginia Baptists to
spread more rapidly throughout the rest of the country
was disappointing as were the continued political bicker-
ing, the civil disorder, and the diplomatic blundering
which threatened the nation's peace and safety. "Such opposition was made to the excise acts in the southern states,"
he wrote in his diary on December 31, 1792, "that President Washington published a proclamation to prevent a
rebellion on September 15, 1792." Two years later, after
the Whiskey rebellion, Backus wrote didactically, "an open

insurrection appeared against our government in the west part of Pennsylvania against whom President Washington marched up with 15,000 men which cost the government not less than a million dollars." A tight-fisted Yankee whose dedication to the Protestant ethic of thrift and hard work was as devout as Benjamin Franklin's, Backus had no use for anything which raised taxes or put the government in such debt as had corrupted Europe, and especially England. One of the prime virtues of Jefferson's administration was a prudence with expenditures that permitted reduction of the national debt.

But foreign affairs, particularly in relation to France, seemed most critically to threaten the nation in the 1790's. Here Backus could indulge his dislike for the Federalists and at the same time take a pietistic view of the world: "Europe is full of confusion and blood," he wrote in 1795; "And are not these the shakings among the nations which God will pursue until the Desire of all Nations shall come? Hag. ii.7." Like the Jeffersonians, Backus considered the British spoliation of American shipping more heinous than that of the French. He firmly believed that America should pursue a policy of peace and avoid any entanglements in the affairs of Europe. So far as the Jeffersonians were the party of peace and the Federalists those who wanted war, he was easily persuaded to be a Jeffersonian.

By the same token, however, he was not willing to join the Jeffersonians in regard to the Jay Treaty. "The war in Europe," he wrote in his diary on December 31, 1795, "drew off a vast quantity of provisions from America, and caused it to flow with money. But our country grew very wanton under their prosperity. The British court in November, 1793, ordered their ships of war to seize American vessels that were bound to or from French ports, which caused many to move in Congress for power to make reprizals upon them. But president Washington sent mr. John Jay as a special agent to England, who produced a treaty with the British court in Novr. 1794, which was ratified by our president and senate in the summer of 1795; and prevented war with Britain. Yet all America was filled with publications against them therefor throughout the year 1795. Thus liberty is made an occasion to the flesh, and a cloak of maliciousness which God has warned us against."

Backus never doubted the benefits of the French Revolution, which was, like that in America, a popular uprising against a tyrannical king to set the people free and to overthrow the ecclesiastical tyranny of a corrupt established church. Backus saw signs of the millennium in the progress of France: "wonderful are the events in Europe," he wrote in 1798: "The French have conquered Rome, and the Pope fled to the island of Malta." Even the establishment of Napoleon as virtual dictator of France in 1798 did not arouse more than this factual comment from him: "Nov. 10, Bonnepatree altered the government of France."

Like Jefferson, Backus chose to remember the French as the "good allies" of America; Hamilton's war policy was base ingratitude. He deplored the tactics used "by our highest rulers as well as others to render" the French "as odious as possible." Congress was planning a war against France while it "continued a strong connection with Britain tho' they took more of our vessels in the year than the French had." Backus put no stock in Jedidiah Morse's fulminations against the conspiracy of the Bavarian Illuminati; the political motives of the established clergy in publicizing this alleged "plot" were too obvious to be taken seriously.

Backus reported happily a year later that "The tide of opinion is again turned in favour of the French nation," but he gave no credit to John Adams for it. Adams, as chief magistrate, "was very fond of partiality," and had done nothing to alter the favored position of the Congregational churches in New England. The fact that Adams split his party and ruined his own political hopes for re-election to preserve peace with France could not alter Backus's opinion that the established politicians and clergy worked hand-in-glove to protect their vested interests.

Beneath the surface of this political antagonism between the Federalist clergy of the established churches and the Jeffersonian Baptists lay a large area of agreement on moral issues. The Baptists, while denying the need for religious taxes, nevertheless insisted as much as the Trinitarian or evangelical "theocrats" like Jedidiah Morse, Timothy Dwight, and later Lyman Beecher, upon the necessity for strict enforcement of the Puritan blue laws and Sabbatarian restrictions. Backus considered it reprehensible that the people of Boston (abetted by the Unitarian infidels and sophisticates who controlled that wicked city) were allowed to defy the laws against theater-going in the 1790's. He noted with grim pleasure in 1798 that the Grand Theater in Boston had burned to the ground "as they were preparing to mimock the burning of Sodom in a play; the fire catched in the house near night and consumed it. . . . A plain testimony against mocking God!" Dwight and Morse fully concurred.

The Baptists also agreed with the evangelical Trinitarian Congregationalists who wanted strict enforcement of laws against profanity, card-playing, gambling, and drunkenness. Backus heartily supported Lyman Beecher's attacks upon dueling after the shooting of Alexander Hamilton: "Such is the madness of man!" he wrote in his diary after the duel. Though Backus did not fear the Democratic or Jacobin Clubs of the 1790's, he disapproved of the Freemasons. "A procession of free masons" passing through the streets of Boston "with a band of music" on the way to Trinity Church "lookt to me more like worshippers of Diana than [of] ye lowly Jesus." His dislike sprang as much from the Masons' association with the

Anglican Church as from their mixture of religion, revelry, and costumes. When they developed a wide following which included many Baptists in rural New England, the Second Baptist Church in Cheshire, Massachusetts voted that "Altho' the Church is ignorant of the Secrecy of Masonry and know not the advantages of that Order, yet for members of this Church to Join them in their Lodges, looks so much like being yoked together with Unbelievers and fellowshipping the Works of Darkness and being unnecessarily Conformed to the World, that the Church agrees to withdraw the right of Fellowship from any Members that frequent the Lodges." In 1798 the Shaftesbury Baptist Association of western Massachusetts and Vermont made membership in Masonry a ground for excommunication. Whether the Baptists feared the Masons for their secrecy or disliked the fact that their activities took the time and money of Christians from religious efforts to prepare for the millennium, there was a general agreement that the organization was anti-Christian. Evangelicals of all denominations joined the great Anti-Masonic Movement that began in 1825, and many Baptists who had formerly been Jeffersonian Democrats became Whigs in the process.

After 1790 both Baptists and evangelical Congregationalists were concerned with associational benevolent activities. By 1783 the Warren Association was urging upon each of the member churches a system of annual subscriptions to support Rhode Island College. The Baptist Education Fund, on which Backus served as a trustee, was incorporated in 1793 by an act of the Massachusetts legislature to raise money to aid needy Baptist students at the College. Three years later the Warren Association expanded its benevolent activities by collecting subscriptions for the aid of indigent ministers' widows. James Manning became involved in a plan to persuade the citizens of Providence to adopt a public school system based upon compulsory taxation of all inhabitants of the city. And shortly after Backus's death in 1806, the New England Baptists began making plans to establish a theological seminary.

The benevolent activity which linked the Baptists most closely to the mainstream of American evangelicalism (and simultaneously marked their steady movement away from radical pietistic sectarianism) were home and foreign missions. The home missions were but the institutionalization of frontier itinerant evangelism. But foreign missions were a significantly new line of endeavor, inspired by English models. William Carey, the founder of the Baptist Missionary Society in England in 1792, gave a tremendous impetus to the idea when he followed the British Empire to India to save the heathen for Christianity. The Baptists of Massachusetts, with Backus's full sympathy, set up their first missionary fund in 1798 primarily for home missionary purposes in the newly settled regions of northern and western New England. But in 1803 the Massachusetts Baptist Missionary Society embarked upon the more ambitious work of foreign missions. To promote this effort the society published a magazine, with Thomas Baldwin, pastor of the Second Baptist Church in Boston, as editor. Backus attended its sessions and was a charter subscriber to its magazine, the first Baptist periodical in America.

In tone and content this magazine was indistinguishable from a dozen other missionary periodicals founded in these years as each denomination vied for public support in the high cause of saving the world. As such it added immeasurably to the respectability and prestige of the Baptists, for in missionary activity the evangelicals found a common cause which lifted them above petty rivalries and dominated Protestantism for the rest of the century.

And in Thomas Baldwin the New England Baptists at last found a man to succeed Backus as the leader of the denomination. Baldwin was born in Bozrah, Connecticut, not far from Norwich, in 1753. His parents were members of the Standing Order, and he remained a Congregationalist until 1780, when two Baptist evangelists in Canaan, New Hampshire (where he had moved in 1769) converted him to antipedobaptism. He joined the Baptist Church and was ordained in 1783. After seven years as a successful evangelist, he was called to the Second Baptist Church in Boston, where he remained until his death in 1826. A man of considerable talent as a writer and speaker, he had served in the New Hampshire legislature before becoming a Baptist preacher, and he always remained a man of public distinction. Though he had no college education, he achieved fame in several controversies over open communion and pedobaptism in the 1790's, was appointed a trustee of the Baptist College in 1794, and received an honorary M.A. that same year. He was elected by the Massachusetts legislature to deliver the annual election sermon in 1802; received an honorary degree of D.D. in 1803 from Union College; and as editor of the Massachusetts Missionary Magazine from 1803 until his death, was the most prominent Baptist minister in New England between Backus and Francis Wayland. Backus, in his declining years, saw the center of the denomination shift from the Providence-Middleborough region (where it had been under his leadership and that of Manning) to the Boston area (under Baldwin, Stillman, and Hezekiah Smith). With the formation of the Boston Baptist Association as the northern division of the Warren Association, this transition was complete.

Backus never complained of this, but reveled in the growing prestige and respectability of the denomination. Nevertheless, to many rural and frontier Baptists, in whom the simpler pietism of the denomination still prevailed, the shift was a matter of serious concern. In 1794 the Shaftesbury Association, representing the churches of western Massachusetts, Vermont, and eastern New York, felt obliged to take cognizance of the problem in a letter to the Warren Association. God had brought great blessings to the United States and to the Baptists; we have "Few enemies, the field maintained, and victory almost won" over persecution by the Standing Order. But new dangers were threatening the denomination. "Our greatest danger," the rural Baptists believed, was that "As we grow numerous, wealthy, learned, and respectable" the denomination may decline in piety. This had happened to other Christian sects in the past and "It will be rare" if the Baptists were to avoid the same temptations to worldliness and pride. The result would be to "diminish in holy zeal, grow formal, and lose the power of religion." If that occurred, then "another Separation must ensue" like that of the new reformation of the 1740's, for "holy souls" will "dissent from our establishment" as we did from that of the Standing Order.

The prediction came true. In 1804 a schism did arise, led by those who believed that the Baptists had become too formal, cold, and worldly. Elder Elias Smith of Portsmouth, New Hampshire, founded a new sect called "The Christians." A series of letters in which he justified this schism named Thomas Baldwin, Hezekiah Smith, Samuel Stillman, and Isaac Backus as men whose "conforming to the world" had produced such spiritual formality that the denomination had become corrupt and lost its spiritual power. Smith urged all pious Baptists to come out and separate themselves from this decadent establishment.

Smith's appeal was somewhat weakened by the fact that he had recently adopted Arminian and Universalist principles, but nevertheless his indictment of the denomination rang true. Smith himself, like Thomas Baldwin, had been born in Connecticut and moved to New Hampshire. He became a Baptist itinerant in 1788 and so impressed Baldwin and Hezekiah Smith by his talents that

they persuaded him to accept a wealthy pastorate in Woburn, on the outskirts of Boston. Baldwin and Samuel Stillman adopted him as their protégé and groomed him for
leadership in the denomination. As he followed their advice
he grew rapidly in wealth and prestige. But, as he later
said in his autobiography, he always felt uneasy about the
compromises the Boston divines forced him to make with
his earlier pietistic principles.

For example, he was shocked to find that Dr. Stillman (he
had been given an honorary D.D. by Rhode Island College in 1788) did not expect any Christian to rise from
his pew and shout "Glory to God!" or "Free grace!" under
the influence of the Spirit. He was surprised to see that in
Baldwin's church there were a large, handsome chan-
delier, "damask curtains," silver candlesticks, and cushions
on the pews. When he first preached there in 1793, Baldwin hinted that he should make his sermon short: "Some
country preachers were apt to speak too long" he said, and
this offended the congregation. When Elias Smith moved
to Woburn, he still wore his old country clothes. But Stillman and Baldwin told him that he must dress in a style
more befitting his position: "They dressed me in black
from head to foot; and on some occasions a part of my dress
was silk with a large three-cornered hat and cloak of the
best. I built a house there; kept a horse and carriage, and
lived in ease as other salary men do. Being so respectable
I began to write my sermons," instead of preaching extemporaneously. He also wore a wig (a custom Backus
himself had adopted in 1770). But what was the final
stroke to him, Stillman insisted that he must wear the
Geneva bands while preaching. Smith asked why this
was so necessary, and Stillman replied, "That as I lived
near the metropolis, it would make me appear respectable;
and besides, said he, it will shew that you are an ordained
minister." When Smith said he feared "We are going back
to the place from whence we came out" in the 1740's,

Baldwin merely answered, "We wish to make our denomination respectable."

Smith's criticisms of Backus were less harsh than those
against Stillman, Baldwin, and Hezekiah Smith. (The
latter, now one of the richest men in Haverhill, had a
congregation which Elias Smith found utterly cold and
formal when he addressed them.) In fact, he praised
Backus for standing up against some of the new practices
which were creeping into the church. Nevertheless he
charged that Backus had made a mistake in accepting an
honorary degree from Rhode Island College in 1797 ("a
desire for titles"), for using this title after his name on
the title pages of his books, and for serving on the Baptist
Education Fund committee (an organization which,
said Smith, had acknowledged the power of the state in
religious affairs by seeking legal incorporation from the
legislature).

It may be said in Backus's defense that he went on record
as opposing the use of the term "Reverend" for Baptist
ministers, preferring, he said, the term "Elder" because
it was a Biblical one. But the question of titles and honorary
degrees was difficult. Up to 1788 Rhode Island College
had awarded honorary degrees of D.D. only to persons in
England. But as the college produced its own learned
ministers, and as educated preachers from the Middle
Colonies arrived, it became impossible to resist the desire
to emulate Harvard and Yale, which honored their eminent men in this way. Samuel Stillman was awarded a
D.D. in 1788 and Hezekiah Smith in 1797, and thereafter
were referred to as "The Reverend Dr. Stillman" and
"The Reverend Dr. Smith." When Union College, which
was Congregational in its support, awarded Baldwin an
honorary D.D. in 1803, the Baptists decided to accept such
titles as their due. It was one of the great ironies of
Backus's life that at the same commencement in which he

received his honorary degree as an accolade for a lifetime of service to the Baptist cause, the college gave an honorary degree to the man who had been one of the foremost opponents of everything Backus had worked for—John Adams, then President of the United States.

Elias Smith did not mention in his attacks upon the declining piety of the Baptists one of the most scandalous episodes of the 1790's—the apparent defection of President Maxcy of Rhode Island College to Universalism. Maxcy, who succeeded Manning as President of the College in 1792, published some tracts in 1796 which aroused considerable alarm among the Baptists. Backus tried to quiet these doubts and then discovered another sermon in which Maxcy praised Joseph Priestley, the Unitarian, as superior in his insights to Jonathan Edwards. Backus, who had known Maxcy from childhood, immediately demanded an explanation. The prestige of the College and the denomination was at stake. "President Edwards had his imperfections," Backus wrote, but to put him "upon a level with Dr. Priestley, who in the most public manner has denied that Christ is truly God, and that he ever made an atonement for the sins of men, must be exceedingly hurtful to young minds and grievous to others." Maxcy replied that his sentiments had been "grossly misrepresented particularly with regard to universalism, a doctrine which I believe contrary to the whole tenor of Scripture." But he did admit that "Some things which I have published were rash and imprudent." Maxcy managed to regain or retain Backus's support and in 1797 was confirmed in his position as President. The situation again revealed the rapidly shifting character of the denomination.

Elias Smith's schism, however, did no serious harm to the denomination. He formed a few congregations here and there, but his Universalism and Arminianism were too heretical to attract the pietists who agreed with his other criticisms. The rural and frontier Baptists were alarmed at some of the revelations he made. He said, for instance, that Thomas Baldwin had departed from Calvinism to the point of preaching the doctrine of General Redemption rather than Particular Redemption. And while he admitted that Stillman vehemently opposed Baldwin on this, he noted that the two men had subordinated their doctrinal differences in the name of harmonious respectability. Smith also attacked the Boston ministers for "foppery," for praying for magistrates from the pulpit, for delivering election sermons at the request of the legislature, for refusing to call the brethren "brother" and "sister." He denounced Baldwin for refusing to let the Negro Baptist minister, Thomas Paul, preach in his pulpit because it would offend his congregation. He called the Warren Baptist Association "hierarchical." And he said that organization of the Baptist Missionary Society was motivated by pride, love of power, and a desire for prestige.

The attack which found the most general response among the rural Baptists, and with which Backus himself thoroughly agreed, was against the trend among the Baptist churches, led by Hezekiah Smith of Haverhill, to seek legal incorporation from the legislature. This problem plagued the Baptists continually after the Cutter Case in 1785, and it divided the denomination during Backus's last years almost as badly as the boycott on certificates which he had urged in 1773.

The obvious reason for incorporation was to comply with the decision in the Cutter case, and thus be sure that religious taxes paid by Baptists would be returned to their ministers by parish or town treasurers. For some Baptists a more compelling reason was to enable a congregation to make binding contracts between its members and its pastor, thereby guaranteeing regular payment of a decent salary. Backus had often criticized his brethren for covetousness in failing to give adequate voluntary support to their pastors, but he could never regard the relationship between a pastor and his flock as a purely civil contract enforceable by law. He viewed the relationship at all levels as purely spiritual. To use the state to collect salaries was as wrong for the Baptists as for the Congregationalists.

Backus also believed that incorporation acknowledged the right of the state to decide which churches could and which could not be chartered. In addition, incorporation gave all persons in the congregation the right to vote on building or repairing a meetinghouse as well as paying the minister's salary. The unconverted members might then be able to outvote the converted, thereby allowing the worldlings to lord it over the saints. Baptist societies, acting like Congregational parishes, would face the same bitter conflicts between church and congregation.

Some Baptists argued that incorporation was necessary to hold property or endowment funds in the name of the church. But Backus pointed out that the law gave the deacons, or any other suitably appointed persons, the power to "receive and hold estates or donations which are given for religious purposes, and to manage the same at the direction and for the good of the church or society." This device was wholly sufficient to meet the needs of the Baptists in this respect.

Backus was of course well aware that in some places the refusal of a Baptist congregation to obtain incorporation meant distraint and imprisonment for those who conscientiously refused to pay religious taxes they might otherwise avoid. On January 20, 1790, three members of the Baptist church in New Gloucester in the District of Maine (then part of Massachusetts) asked his advice on precisely this issue. They had only a part-time minister and the town had decided that this did not qualify them for exemption. It threatened "a Law Suit unless we will Petition to the General Court to be set off a Society by our selves; this they are in General Very willin for and as we now stand according to the Constitution they must rate us Say they. Now Sir Would you Advise us to Petition the General Court or Not?" Backus unquestionably wished them not to seek incorporation and to suffer the consequences. However, they did petition the legislature and secured incorporation.

The annual meeting of the Warren Association in September, 1791, learned that two Baptist societies had sought incorporation, but that Samuel Stillman had persuaded them to withdraw their petitions and seek advice from the Association. Backus spoke vigorously for a resolution against incorporation, while Hezekiah Smith spoke in favor of letting each church make its own decision on the matter. Backus won the day and the association resolved "That it be earnestly commended to the churches belonging to this association by no means to apply to civil government for incorporation. . . . because we cannot consent to blend the kingdom of Christ with the kingdoms of this world nor to support it by the power of the civil magistrates."

But Hezekiah Smith's congregation refused to follow this recommendation. In 1793 the Haverhill Baptists petitioned for and secured incorporation. Backus angrily brought the matter before the Association, which once again voted its disapproval. But resolutions could not settle the problem. In 1798 the Baptist churches in Harwich and Brookfield followed Haverhill's example, as did Ashfield in 1800. Over the next decade a score of other Baptist churches successfully sought the same privilege. In most of these cases the action was justified on the grounds that this was the only way to avoid paying religious taxes to the establishment.

Backus did not live to see the final resolution of this problem in the passage of the "Religious Liberty Act" of 1811, which reversed the Cutter Case by interpreting Article Three as applying to all churches, incorporated or unincorporated.

Backus had few other occasions in the last years of his life to be concerned with the problem of Church-State relations. Except for a thorny situation involving religious taxes in Harwich and Barnstable, which dragged on through the 1790's without ever resulting in any petition to the legislature, nothing significant came before the Grievance Committee. "Very few of them," he wrote of the parishes in 1796, "now dare to make distress upon any who refuse to pay ministers' taxes." He did ride to Hartford in 1791 to deliver a forceful assault upon the ecclesiastical system in Connecticut to an audience of Baptists and their sympathizers, who were then waging a vigorous campaign for disestablishment.

For the most part Backus returned, after 1790, to his old activities as an itinerant evangelist and denominational trouble-shooter. From 1790 to 1797 he annually rode over 1,100 miles on horseback throughout New England, delivering an average of 150 sermons each year and participating in numerous councils. Still, his efforts to produce in New England the same kind of religious fervor which he had seen in Virginia proved futile. Seldom did he note any "moving of the Spirit" or "descent of the power" in the meetings he addressed. Most depressing of all, he was unable to arouse any stirring among the "dry bones" in his own congregation.

Regularly he noted in his diary and "Bills of Mortality" the deaths of old friends and stalwarts who had fought side by side with him in the early years of persecution and adversity—days to which he looked back fondly now for the exhilarating spiritual fervor which had animated the young denomination. It almost seemed as though religion throve better under persecution than in the "tolerating times" after 1790. In 1801 he noted sadly that only fourteen persons were still alive among the sixty-one who had joined the Separate Church in Middleborough during the first ten months after it was founded in 1747/ 48, and only five of these were still living in the town and attending his church.

His activities for the denomination now were largely institutional—attending association meetings, participating in the college corporation, raising funds and making policies for the Baptist Education Fund, promoting the missionary movement. In 1795 he helped to form a new circulating library in Middleborough. In April, 1797, he had a portrait made of himself (wearing his large white wig and looking very round in the face); he did so at the request of his English friend, John Rippon, who wanted to print it in his Baptist Annual Register as a tribute to the elder statesman.

Despite the spiritual dullness of the times, Backus kept his faith in the rapid advance of the millennium. "The credit of the Baptist churches and ministers is daily rising in all parts of our country," he wrote in 1796. And he noted with eager anticipation that the Jews of Europe seemed to be on the verge of conversion to Christianity: "the Jews have appointed a Congress at Amsterdam next month," he wrote on July 15, 1794, "to examine the Scriptures to find whether Jesus is the true Messiah or not. A glorious event!" He had no doubt what such an examination would reveal, but apparently the conference never materialized.

As he reached his last years he assumed the position of a patriarch in his community. The following description of him by a Congregational neighbor reveals vividly the impact he had upon those who heard him preach in the 1790's:

Mr. Backus was of a large, robust and muscular frame, made firm, probably, by his early agricultural labours, and by his travels on horseback, the greater part of his life. His large face and head appeared more venerable by reason of his very large wig, an adornment of ministers in the times in which he lived. . . . His sermons were marked by strong good sense and often striking thought and were generally of a highly biblical character. Few men make so strong an impression upon their audience by personal appearance as he did. His venerable countenance, his large features, his imposing wig, in which he always appeared in the pulpit, his impressing gravity and deep toned voice, added to the weight of his sentiment, gave him great power over an audience.

In 1798, at the age of seventy-four, his health took a turn for the worse. He had been troubled since 1793 with "a soreness and swelling in my private parts" which stemmed from prostate inflammation. On February 11, 1798, "My old disorder came on so in the week past, and was so great today, that I did not preach, which is the first sabbath that I have been hindered therefrom by bodily illness in 38 years." In 1798 he rode only 358 miles and this total decreased steadily thereafter until in 1802 he was able to travel only twenty miles and deliver twenty-eight sermons during the whole year.

He tried various cures suggested by doctors. In December, 1800, he underwent "a course of mercury physic" which lasted for a week but brought no relief. Later he tried "annointing with sulphur." But there was no cure short of surgery and apparently no one suggested that to him.

His inactivity enforced by illness became doubly hard when signs of a revival of religious excitement began after 1800 in New England. On Dec. 31, 1801, he noted in his diary, "Although stupidity has greatly prevailed in our land, yet religion has been revived in many places. 33 have

been added to the two baptist churches in Boston, 34 to
that in Wrentham, 33 to the first in Attleboro, 38 in Woodstock, 29 to Harvard, 47 to Providence, 62 to elder Hicks's
in Rehoboth, and 100 in Dighton in the year past, and the
like in many other places. And by a letter from Georgia of
Nov. 17, 1801, it is said, 'According to the best account
from Kentucky, there has been added to the baptist
churches since last march near 6000 while multitudes
were joining to the methodists and presbyterians.' "

Despite his growing incapacity, his congregation bore
with him patiently and lovingly, though they were frequently forced to go many weeks without services because
he was unable to travel even the short distance from his
home to the meetinghouse. Finally, in the fall of 1804, the
church, noting that "the infirmities of Old Age" had over-
taken their pastor, voted to call a younger man to assist
him. Ezra Kendall, then thirty-two years old, had preached
in the church on trial for the two months preceding this
call, and doubtless Backus approved of it. Kendall had no
education but had been licensed to preach in 1798 and
from 1802 to 1803 had served the Baptist Church in
Martha's Vineyard. It was apparently understood that he
would succeed Backus. Meanwhile he preached part of
the time to another Baptist congregation in Kingston,
Rhode Island.

Backus had the satisfaction of seeing this young preacher
at last succeed in accomplishing what he had tried in vain
to do. The Middleborough First Baptist Church began to
show signs of a revival. Thirteen persons were converted
in the fall of 1804 and ten more by August of 1805. But
Backus's rejoicing was marred by doubts about Kendall's
orthodoxy. The younger man, like many other Calvinists,
seemed tainted with Arminianism.

Matters came to a head early in January, 1805, when
Backus heard Kendall, talking to the congregation on a Sat-

urday night, deliberately attack some of the basic tenets of the faith. The old pastor at once wrote him: "Your attempt last Saturday evening, by reading a harsh pamphlet to force me from my faith about original righteousness and original sin, and treating my ideas contemptuously, tended to alienate my mind from you." Kendall was trying to argue against the popular view that Calvinistic predestination was nothing more than fatalism or determinism. To do so he was willing to modify the strict Calvinist view which declared men so totally depraved as a result of Adam's fall that their damnation was justified even if they committed no sins themselves. The crux of the matter in this dispute centered upon the old issue of infant damnation. This ancient question aroused new interest and excitement at the turn of the century because of the increasingly optimistic and perfectionist temper of American life and the general acceptance of the empirical epistemology of John Locke. If all men, all children, were born with a mind which was a *tabula rasa,* a blank sheet of paper on which experience would write all that they could ever know, then the child must come into the world as a wholly new, fresh, and innocent creature. The theological shift from the Calvinistic conception of the Deity as a God of Wrath, an arbitrary, inscrutable Sovereign of the Universe, to the evangelical conception of the Deity as a God of Benevolence, a loving Father to mankind, made it increasingly difficult to sustain the view that he would send infants to roast in hell for the sins of Adam. In addition, the evangelical doctrine of free grace and the evangelical practice of experimental religion were placing more and more emphasis upon the role of man in turning from sin, repenting of sin, and accepting Christ on faith. Backus might call it Arminianism to preach as though men were somehow capable of doing something to save themselves, yet ever since the first tour of George Whitefield, more and more people had been construing New Light preaching in these terms.

Infant damnation therefore brooked large in popular theology in the opening years of the nineteenth century. It was ultimately resolved against Calvinism in favor of the innocence of childhood. Backus held out to the end, yet even he preferred to beg the question. He virtually conceded the argument against Calvinism by regretfully reducing it to an unfathomable mystery: "What God does with all who die in infancy he has not informed us; and the horrid idea of damnation to them, which has been held up by some, serves only to inflame the passions against the plain words of revelation." As for predestination, all men were "children of wrath . . . born with a disposition to love self above God," yet he also insisted that "each soul who truly repents of sin and believes in the Son of God shall be saved from wrath through him." The argument boiled down to the question of how the soul "truly repents and believes." Backus and Kendall agreed that the agency of God or the Holy Spirit was necessary. But neither they, nor any of the evangelicals in the next thirty years, resolved the relationship between the agency of man and the agency of God in creating the circumstances in which the Holy Spirit would be disposed to take the initiative. Somehow the initiative seemed more and more to lie with man to open the door at which a benign and waiting Christ sought entrance.

It is significant that Backus offered as the ultimate test of the validity of his interpretation of Scripture the argument that "These ideas are confirmed by the experience of sixty three years." Unfortunately for Backus's Calvinism, the experience of the Arminians in the Second Great Awakening was to prove just as convincing to them. However much Backus was shocked by Kendall's views, his congregation evidently found them acceptable. Kendall held the pulpit until a year after Backus's death, when he resigned to become pastor of the Baptist Church in Kingston.

Though illness and old age kept Backus from traveling much after 1798, he continued to write and publish. He was almost as delighted with the election of Thomas Jefferson in 1800 as he was with the new wave of revivals throughout the nation; in his mind the two events were part of the same reformation, which had begun in 1740 and which would end (in the not too distant future) with the millennium. On April 20, 1805, he wrote to Elder William Richards in England, "The liberty that he [Roger Williams] was for, civil and religious, is now enjoyed in thirteen of the seventeen of the United States of America. No tax for any religious minister is imposed by authority in any of the said 13 States, and their power is much weakened in the other 4. Slavery is also abolished in the northern States and it is wearing away in the rest. And since Mr. Jefferson became President in 1801 our national debt has been much diminished and last March he was elected again into that office by 162 votes when there was but 14 for any other man. And he has been gaining in esteem in the minds of people."

One great blow marred his old age—the death of his wife, Susanna, in 1800, five days before what would have been their fifty-first wedding anniversary. She had been bedridden for two months with what Backus called "jaundice and dropsy in her stomach." The entry in the diary reveals his grief and her own characteristically quiet endurance: "Nov. 24, a heavy day. My wife said not a great deal about dying. Elder Rathbun was here on the 12th. and prayed with her, and when he asked her what she would have him pray for, she said, 'I am not so much concerned about living or dying, as to have my will swallowed up in the will of God.' . . . For many weeks she could take no hearty food, and rarely took any drink without vomitting after it, and she had much inward pain, but bore it with great patience, and never expressed any fears of death. Thus she wasted away until about six o'clock this morning, when she expired without any great struggles."

In March, 1806, Backus suffered a stroke which paralyzed one of his arms. Still, he felt well enough on April 3 to enter the pulpit and preach. It was his last sermon. Twenty days later he suffered a second stroke from which he never recovered. His speech failed and he lingered on, paralyzed, until November 20. A man who lived in Middleborough and often heard him preach, though himself a Congregationalist, provided an appropriate comment on his life: "Mr. Backus was called 'Father' not only by his own people, who might well thus honour him, but by almost the entire community; and a Patriarch he was, not only by ecclesiastical powers, but as a Pastor and Divine, and in moral power and weight of well-earned and well-established character."

Fifty years after his death, a historical society was founded in his name which utilized his collected papers and books as the basis for a library of Baptist history in New England. In 1893 a marble memorial was erected over his grave in Middleborough by his denomination to commemorate his "zeal and industry in the cause of civil and religious liberty."

But Backus's importance lies beyond his relationship to his denomination or to the movement to separate Church and State. It lies in his almost perfect embodiment of the evangelical spirit of his times. Greater men than he expressed the theological, the political, the Enlightenment views of the latter part of the eighteenth century—Edwards, Jefferson, Franklin. But few men expressed so well in thought and action that vigorous, fervent, conscientious, experimental pietism which constituted the fundamental spirit of the new nation and which made its experiment in freedom unique.

EPILOGUE
The New Light
and the Enlightenment

"*[The Standing Order] compares our separation
to a rebellion against the* STATE." ISAAC BACKUS, *A
Fish Caught* (1767) p. 23.

THE TAPROOT of the American temper is pie-
tism. Puritanism is one form of pietism, but it is not the
strain which has predominated in the United States of
America. The predominant strain has been the evangelical form which originated among the eighteenth century
Separate-Baptists, whose foremost leader was Isaac Backus.

The eighteenth century Baptist movement grew out of
the Great Awakening, the point at which the colonies shed
the medieval concept of a corporate Christian society
which the English had brought with them from the Old
World. In his career and writings Backus helped to create
the new national ethos which emerged after 1775 and
which Edmund Burke rightly described as "the dissidence
of dissent and the protestantism of the Protestant religion." The evangelical movement laid the groundwork
for the Revolution. It played a major role in the breakdown of the static, aristocratic, class-stratified, and carefully controlled social order of the old colonial society.

The Awakening has often been misinterpreted as a conservative, backward-looking reaction against the new philosophical outlook of the Enlightenment. It was, in fact, a very dynamic part of the new orientation in Western thought. The experimental pietism of the revival was a radical departure from the old Puritan conception of man's relationship to God and to society. The Baptists embodied this new religious outlook in its most vital and enduring form; a form which ultimately gave the tone to all American religion. They thought of their "experimental" religion in terms which to them were just as inductive and scientific as the discoveries of Newton, Boyle, or Locke. Experimental piety was therefore the competitor of deistic rationalism in capturing the minds of enlightened Americans. It stated in religious terms what the Enlightenment philosophers wanted to state primarily in humanistic, secular, or rationalistic terms. Isaac Backus, the most prolific and effective writer for the Baptist movement in the century, clearly expressed the scientific "doctrines of grace" and thereby provided a more viable alternative to deism than the Puritanism of Cotton Mather or than the new "liberal Christianity" of Unitarianism.

The most striking feature of the radical pietism of the New Light evangelicalism was its doctrine of separation of Church and State. Here too the Baptist movement took the lead and Isaac Backus was the foremost exponent. The movement to grant full religious equality to all sects sprang in part from the practical position of the New Light dissenters within the tax-supported established church systems of Puritanism and Anglicanism. But more important, it sprang from the resurgence of the pietistic doctrines of the priesthood of all believers and of the gathered, voluntaristic church—a resurgence which stemmed directly from the repudiation of a learned ministry and a hierarchical or presbyterian polity. Here the evangelical pietism of the Baptists ran into direct conflict with and demolished the increasingly stratified Puritanism of the eighteenth century. Puritanism had always been socially conservative in its insistence upon moral order. The Baptist doctrines stressed the egalitarianism, the rampant individualism, and the perfectionist concept of majority rule which formed the basis of the American "experiment in republican government" after 1775. Experimental religion and Jeffersonian republicanism merged in the Revolutionary era to form the quintessence of the new nation. Both contained a fundamental belief in the freedom and trustworthiness of the conscience, "the moral sense," of the common man; both held to the concept of a benevolent God interested in the happiness of his children; and both were convinced of the millennial mission of America—the hope of the world. The Scottish Realists eventually systematized the theological and philosophical assumptions of these views, but only after the evangelicals and the Jeffersonian rationalists in the American laboratory provided the experimental basis for their conclusions.

Isaac Backus supplied the fervent appeals as well as the logical rationale for the Baptist movement, in the same way that Thomas Jefferson supplied these qualities for the political movement of the incipient republic. And it is not surprising that both men considered as among their prime achievements their efforts to separate Church and State. Jefferson looked forward to the creation of a secular state based upon the rationalistic religion of the French Enlightenment. Backus looked forward to the creation of a Christian society based upon the evangelical view of man's relationship to God and His laws. To understand Isaac Backus as a man, as a Baptist, as an exponent of American evangelical pietism is therefore more profoundly to understand the whole nature of the American temper.

A Note on the Sources

THE BASIC primary source for this book has been the large collection of papers left by Isaac Backus, notably his diary, autobiography, travel journals, letters, and miscellaneous denominational manuscripts. Scattered in several libraries, the great bulk of these are at Andover Newton Theological School in Newton Center, Massachusetts. But the gift of Backus papers to Brown University by Miss Florence Backus in 1963 has greatly enriched its collection. Mrs. Elliot Perkins of Middleborough, Massachusetts also has a valuable group of Backus papers handed down in the family. There are additional Backus papers at the American Antiquarian Society, the Rhode Island Historical Society, the Massachusetts Historical Society, the Boston Public Library, the New York Public Library, the Houghton Library at Harvard University, the Haverford College Library, the American Baptist Historical Society in Rochester, New York, the British Museum in London, and the Angus Library in Oxford. A complete letterpress edition of the unpublished papers of Isaac Backus is currently being prepared for publication by the Brown University Press under a grant from the National Historical Publications Commission in Washington, D.C. For a useful but old calendar of the Backus Papers see William H. Allison, *Inventory of Unpublished Material for American Religious History in Protestant Church Archives and Other Repositories* (Washington, 1910) pp. 39-54.

In addition, the state and county archives in Massachusetts and Connecticut as well as many town and church records provided much important material in legislative records, petitions, memorials, affidavits, and legal records. The Massachusetts Ecclesiastical Archives and Superior Court files in Boston and the county court records have been especially useful. Baptist church records for the eighteenth century are difficult to find and are often still in the local churches or in private hands, but there are some at Andover Newton Theological School, the American Baptist Historical Society, the Vermont Baptist Historical Society (now in the state historical society at Montpelier) and the Connecticut State Archives in Hartford. The records of Backus's Baptist Church are in the possession of the Backus Memorial Church in Middleborough.

Valuable material on the Separates and Baptists can also be found in many Congregational church records and state historical societies. The best collections of papers on the Separates are in the Connecticut Historical Society in Hartford and the New London County Historical Society in New London. The records of Backus's Separate church in Titicut are at Andover Newton Theological School. The Rhode Island Historical Society and the Newport Historical Society have important Baptist materials relating to Backus's career. The records of the First Congregational Church in Norwich are in the Connecticut State Archives.

Extant papers of other eighteenth century Baptist leaders are few. Those of Morgan Edwards and Hezekiah Smith are the most notable and these are widely scattered. Brown University has its own official records and some of James Manning's papers. The Brown Family Papers at the John Carter Brown Library in Providence contain some valuable items, as do the Ezra Stiles Papers at Yale and the John Adams and Robert Treat Paine Papers at Massachusetts Historical Society.

Of almost equal importance as sources for this book have been the works published by Backus and his contemporaries. Good bibliographies of Backus's works are contained in Thomas B. Maston's *Isaac Backus, Pioneer of Religious Liberty* (Rochester, 1962) and in Milton V. Backman's unpublished doctoral dissertation, "Isaac Backus: A Pioneer Champion of Religious Liberty," University of Pennsylvania, 1959. I am currently preparing an anthology of several of these tracts for the John Harvard Library series. Backus's four volumes of Baptist history, based largely on his own experiences, was edited with valuable notes by David Weston in 1871. Backus's polemical disputes with Benjamin Lord, Joseph Fish, Israel Holly, and Ebenezer Frothingham are full of revealing insights into the history and outlook of the participants in the Great Awakening. The works of Separates like Frothingham, Holly, and Solomon Paine supply their side of the story, but few of the Separate-Baptists besides Backus published significant works. There is virtually nothing published by Manning, Stillman, Hezekiah Smith, or John Davis which throws any light on Backus's career. The autobiography of Elias Smith (Portsmouth, N.H., 1816), quoted extensively in Chapter IX, is of considerable interest however. See also Edward C. Starr, *A Baptist Bibliography* (Philadelphia, 1947-).

Two important primary sources which cannot be listed in detail are of course the newspapers of the day, in which much of the controversy over Church and State took place, and the annual minutes published by the various Baptist Associations, especially those of the Warren Association, which detail not only statistical growth but also changing attitudes and activities on all issues of importance to the Baptists. Many of the original manuscripts of the Warren Association are among the Backus Papers at Andover Newton Theological School including Backus's unpublished history of it.

The only published biography of Backus is that by Alvah Hovey (Boston, 1859). Milton V. Backman's thesis, mentioned above, is based upon the Backus Papers and provides a useful supplement to Hovey. Thomas Maston's thesis, "The Ethical and Social Attitudes of Isaac Backus," Yale, 1939 (shortened considerably for publication) offers a good general analysis of his ideas, but it is not a biography. The best biographical sources on Backus's circle are two by Reuben A. Guild, *Early History of Brown University Including the Life,*

Times, and Correspondence of President Manning (Providence, 1897) and *Chaplain Smith and the Baptists* (Philadelphia, 1885). Valuable information can also be found in volume six of William B. Sprague's *Annals of the American Pulpit* (New York, 1860) and David Benedict's *A General History of the Baptist Denomination* (Boston, 1813). There are histories of the Baptists in the various states and histories of the various denominations which provide useful information of varying quality. The best general history of the Baptists in America is still that of Albert H. Newman (New York, 1894).

The general literature on the Great Awakening is too large to note here. By far the best treatment of the Baptists' part in it is that by Clarence C. Goen, *Revivalism and Separatism in New England, 1740-1800* (New Haven, 1962). Goen is concerned primarily with theological and ecclesiastical issues rather than separation of Church and State. An excellent local study of the Awakening is John M. Bumsted, "The Pilgrims' Progress: The Ecclesiastical History of Southeastern Massachusetts, 1620-1776," unpublished doctoral dissertation, Brown University, 1965. The best discussion of Church-State issues is that provided by L. K. Wroth and H. B. Zobel in the *Legal Papers of John Adams* (Cambridge, 1965) II, 20-46. The older studies of this question by M. L. Greene, P. E. Lauer, R. J. Purcell, J. F. Thorning, S. H. Cobb, D. B. Ford, Jacob C. Meyer, and Susan M. Reed are uneven, inaccurate, and dated.

Local histories, if carefully used, often provide valuable information and insights into the role of the Separate-Baptists in the latter part of the eighteenth century, but these are too numerous to list here. Still I must acknowledge my debt to the following which have been drawn up for this book: Frances M. Caulkins, *History of Norwich, Connecticut* (Norwich, 1845); Ellen D. Larned, *History of Windham County, Connecticut* (Worcester, 1874); Frederick Denison, *Notes on the Baptists and Their Principles in Norwich, Connecticut* (Norwich, 1857); Thomas Weston, *History of the Town of Middleboro, Massachusetts* (Boston, 1906); Arthur E. Wilson, *Wey-*

bosset Bridge in Providence Plantations (Boston, 1947); George F. Clark, *History of the Town of Norton, Massachusetts* (Boston, 1859); John Daggett, *A Sketch of the History of Attleborough, Massachusetts* (Boston, 1894); William L. Chaffin, *History of the Town of Easton, Massachusetts* (Cambridge, 1886); Frederick G. Howes, *History of the Town of Ashfield, Massachusetts* (n.p., n.d.); J. E. A. Smith, *History of Pittsfield, Massachusetts* (Boston, 1869), and George Partridge, *History of the Town of Bellingham, Massachusetts* (Bellingham, 1919).

And finally, there are two works of special importance which fit into no category: Williston Walker, *The Creeds and Platforms of Congregationalism* (New York, 1893) and Samuel Eliot Morison, "Struggle over the Adoption of the Constitution of Massachusetts," Massachusetts Historical Society *Proceedings,* L (1917) 353-411. The best general study of the Awakening and its aftermath is Alan Heimert, *Religion and the American Mind* (Cambridge, 1966) which unfortunately did not come into my hands until this book was in page proof.

Index